A Book of Fables
CLEVER FOXES & LUCKY KLUTZES

WILLIAM J. O'MALLEY, S.J.

TABOR®
PUBLISHING

Allen, Texas

Illustrations by John McDearmon

Send all inquiries to:
Tabor Publishing
200 East Bethany Drive
Allen, Texas 75002-3804

Printed in the United States of America

ISBN 0-7829-0364-9

1 2 3 4 5   97 96 95 94 93

CONTENTS

This book is for
NICHOLAS LOMBARDI, S.J.,
tirelessly generous wizard.

INTRODUCTION

Some truths are simply too enormous to capture in ironclad treatises: love, honor, passion, freedom, heart-weariness. Trying to cram a rhino into pram.

My dictionary takes 42 lines to define "love," and after all that precision, I sighed, "I wish I knew as little about love as that Webster." As Saint Exupery said, "The essential is always invisible." But a muddy kid in a doorway, with a fistful of dandelions, says love, too. And a lot better.

The great human truths are inescapable, and yet elusive. So for centuries, tribes gathered by the fire to try to make sense of their struggles to live with dignity by telling stories of those who discovered—painfully—what human living is for. Evil was compacted into dragons and griffins (often in disguise), but it was always an evil that could be overcome by courage and tenacity . . . and luck.

So, I invite you to hunker here by my fire and enter through the flames into a world where weak princes can turn into brave bears and damsels need not resort to swooning but stand up to be counted. You might find the world we resign ourselves to could really be more like that world.

TENDER IS THE KNIGHT

nce upon a time, long, long ago, when thinking for yourself was considered only babysteps short of blasphemy, there was this seedy knight school for the sons of seedy aristocrats called Bloquehedd Hall near the town of Lowbrough in Dumcoughshire. The philosophy of the school was unyieldingly pragmatic. As the headmaster, Sir Buncombe Blunderbus—himself an alumnus and everything Bloquehedd stood for—told parents on prize days, "Bloquehedd Hall stands four-square behind the old values: an obedient mind in an obedient body!"

Consistent with that purpose, there would be no hint at Bloquehedd Hall of what Sir Buncombe called "sissy bilge," such as wearing out a perfectly good set of eyes poring through dusty books or spinning out strings of numbers like old women knitting air. No, Sir Buncombe guaranteed real Bloquehedd *men.* Thus his lads labored from well before dawn to well after dusk honing the only three skills real men need: brawn, cunning, and an unyielding narrow-mindedness in regard to dragons.

Upon arrival, each new boy received a baby calf which he was enjoined to dead-lift from the ground over his head 50 times daily. As a result, if the boys managed to survive until their final year, even those in danger of failing could lift a Brahma bull to arm's length in the air as effortlessly as a kitten. Later in the morning, they trussed themselves into great iron boilers with pots over their heads and ran briskly at one another, attempting to gore or concuss or at least befuddle their opponents with metal-tipped vaulting poles. After a brief siesta or an opportunity to consult the surgeon, they practiced creeping up on one another in the forest, carefully scrutinizing an opponent's weaknesses in order to batter him senseless. Then march, march, march with measured tread for two hours—as if even a senile dragon could not hear them coming from a league away. Not to mention that they were totally exhausted upon arrival and unable even to raise a sword. After a spartan supper, two hours of indoctrination followed regarding the armaments, tactics, and perfidies of the pernicious dragons who were their path to perpetuity, concluding with five minutes of screeched insults against their scaly foes: "Blowhards!" the aspirants shrieked. "Spawn of Eve's Enemy! Serrated putrescences! Dung-brained dingbats!" Prizes were awarded for ardor, inventiveness, and sweat. And at nine the boys fell to their cots, stuporous.

But the best-laid plans often fail to factor fractiousness into the formula. Among the transfers this spring was a boy named Percival Wemyck McCorkindale, whom his few friends called "Corky" and to whom his exasperated masters referred as "Prissy." It seems young McCorkindale obstinately refused to grow enthusiastic about the activities for which red-blooded males were providentially destined. So finally the masters sent the young reprobate to the headmaster, which Bloquehedd boys opined was as close as one got to a dry-run with a dragon.

"Come *in,* you insolent young *puppy!*" Sir Buncombe tended to roar, quite often in italics. And Corky stood before the huge uncluttered desk, knees shuddering and eyes flaring like a calf in a burning barn. "Your *masters* tell me that you are most unpro*fess*ional, un*teach*able, and un-*Bloquehedd!* Half-hearted lifts; first one to clang butt-down in jousts; constantly crept up on and thrashed; and you shriek dragon insults no better than a mewling *girl!* Not a droplet of sweat! Do you have a *death-wish* or something? *Explain* yourself!"

"Well, Sir," Corky said, "I . . . I don't like hurting people."

"*Wha-a-a-a-a-t?*" Sir Buncombe inquired.

"And the dragons, sir. I've never heard anybody except our village drunk say they've ever even seen a dragon. And if we've never met one, how do we know they aren't . . . nice?"

"*Wha-a-a-a-a-t?*" Sir Buncombe tended to repeat himself.

"Perhaps it's genetic, sir. My father was a philosopher."

"But your father sent you *here!* To become a *man!*"

"My father's dead, sir."

"Then who . . . ?"

"My mother's brother, sir. Sir Crassley Biggott. He's . . ."

". . . the *greatest* manufacturer of armaments in the kingdom," Sir Buncombe concluded. "*And* an illustrious alumnus of this institution! *And* a most generous benefactor, without whose . . ." The headmaster's black brows bushed over the bridge of his nose. "Oh, no you don't, young *scalawag!* You will not fail out of this school so you can read *novels* all day! You will not be the maverick who proves me an incompetent! You will not deprive me . . . this *school* . . . of 50,000 ducats a year!"

"I'll try to be more . . . dedicated, sir."

"Oh, no, you rap*scall*ion! Who knows which of those numbwit masters has already written to your uncle? They're all after my head*master*ship! If not my head. No, no! We must have an . . . an incontestable *triumph! Today!* Or at least before the mails go out tomorrow. *Out* of here! This *instant!* Go out and skin a dragon and bring it back to me, by *breakfast!*"

"But . . ."

"Not a word! And if you fail . . ." The headmaster leaned down to Corky's melting face. "If you fail, you will run the gauntlet! Do . . . or die! Either is perfectly acceptable."

So, utterly wretched, Percival Wemyck McCorkindale turned toward the door and headed toward the forest, in despair.

Meanwhile, up in their wooded lair, the young dragons were committed to self-improving activities not unlike those of their punier counterparts below. Each morning they practiced breathing fire and belching smoke, which left the eyes, ears, noses, and throats of many of the less hardy as parched as a blasted heath. Afternoons, they practiced lopping the heads off trees with their great green tails, or butting one another blithery in headlong charges, or spreading their great leathern wings and soaring out to divebomb villagers on their way to market. These predations were never reported, since the villagers did not want their neighbors to believe them balmy. No other harm came to them since, unbeknownst to the peasants, the dragons were resolute vegetarians.

Like their armored enemies in the valley, the young dragons occupied evenings with indoctrination regarding the armaments, tactics, and perfidies of the pernicious knights, also concluding with five minutes of screeched insults against their sworn foes: "Potheads!" the aspirants roared. "Spawn of Eve! Hairy hogs! Beer-bellied boobs!" And at nine the young dragons sprawled out like deflated green dirigibles, stuporous.

Among these fledgling legends was Barnaby Kraken Typhon, popular with his mates for his glad heart and willingness to plod onward even when it seemed backward to do so. Unfortunately, he had captured the single-minded ardor of a red dragonette named Jessica, cheerleader at the weekly contests where the dragons endeavored with fire and fang to achieve immortality.

As children, Barnaby and Jessica had played with the rest of their companions, and Jessica took no more notice of him than any other of the clumsy and oafish males. But ever since the spring moulting, she had begun to lurk about more inescapably than a process server, batting her fan-rake lashes and cooing rapturously at Barnaby such embarrassing things as: "When I look at those enormous muscles coiling under that green silken skin I could *die*." And Barnaby dearly wished she would.

Today, however, had been too much even for his long-suffering patience. At the end of maneuvers, before the whole platoon, Jessica had attached herself to Barnaby, clinging to his great green shoulders and refusing dislodgement till he swore himself hers alone unto eternity, and so forth and so on. As Barnaby trudged red-faced through the hoots and snorts of his classmates, Jessica stood woebegone by a fire-blasted oak, a single tear dribbling down her crimson cheek, wondering at the unfairness of life in general and games-mad males in particular.

That very evening, Barnaby crept from the camp into the forest and wandered aimlessly until he found a grove, curved round himself, and fell asleep. So exhausted was he that he did not hear, an hour later, the bushes around the grove rustle, nor see a boy stumble forward and collapse wearily at his side.

Corky had not seen even a hint of dragons. For all he cared, there were no dragons. He had made up his mind. Once he had gotten some sleep, he would run away and join the circus. So he lay down his sword and shield and slumped next to a gray-green rock, still warm from the spring sun, and he fell asleep.

Next morning, dawn rose slowly in the sky like a roseate maiden from her couch. Starlings began to chirp, flickers to trill, bluebirds to chortle, whippoorwills to warble, bobolinks to cackle, and in general they set up a considerable avian racket. Barnaby stirred toward wakefulness, and Corky sat up stiff as a bookend, eyes glaring. The rock against which he'd slept was . . . moving! Barnaby felt something stir at his flank and slowly, slowly arced his great head around. His yellow eyes popped big as ostrich eggs at the boy staring open-mouthed back at him.

"One of *them!!!*" they both gasped in unison.

Ever so slowly, Barnaby began to slither toward one side of the grove and Corky toward the other. But when they reached the bushline, they slowly turned and looked at one another, each trying to fit this miraculous apparition somewhere into the thicket of propaganda each carried in his head.

Corky grinned hesitantly back over his shoulder. "Hee, uh, hee-hee. Uh, live and let live, that's what I always say."

"Well," Barnaby shrugged, showing the full length and breadth and depth of his rows of lethal teeth, "I'd

. . . uh . . . be the last one to be . . . uh . . . the first one to . . . ha-ha-ha."

"My name's Corky," the boy said, getting up and dusting the dirt and leaves from his clothes.

"Barnaby," the dragon said and tried to reorient his parts without cutting the boy off at the knees.

"This is, uh . . ." Corky shuffled from foot to foot. "Quite a *coincidence.* I, uh . . . I'm in a bit of disgrace back at school."

"Me, too," Barnaby blushed.

"They think I'm a coward . . . or even unfanatic. So you see, uh, I was sent out to redeem myself by . . . by . . . well, actually, uh, slaughtering one of you guys and bringing back your skin."

"Really."

"Yep. That's it," Corky smiled, swinging his arms back and forth to get the nerves out of them. "You can see my sword and shield, uh, there in the middle, uh, where I can't get at them."

"I see. My case is worse. There's a . . . well, I think you call them 'girls.' Gone goofy about me, and, well, I just ran away in shame. Now I'm going to look even more of a fool when I go back."

"Well, you are a really fine dragon specimen. Better than the pictures they show us. Strings of drool hanging from these big rubbery mouths. Not you, though. Really handsome."

"You think so?"

"Absolutely."

"Great trophy in the old school museum, eh?"

Corky shuffled. "Well, yes. But I mean, no. I mean," he chuckled, "I don't exactly see you and me mixing it up, I mean, like, uh, *mano a mano,* eh? You, uh, don't, uh, either . . . do you?"

Barnaby cocked a squint around an idea. "You know, I might have a solution to both our problems. You see, it's springtime."

"Yes, I, uh, noticed."

"And in springtime, we dragons moult."

"Moult? Is that like what you make beer out of?"

"No. Moult. We shed our skins."

"Very interesting. But . . ." His eyes went wide. "I *see!*"

"And we dump them in a cave just over there," Barnaby said. "You can have as many as you like. Come back for more, anytime."

Corky's face split into an enormous grin, and the long stilettoes of Barnaby's teeth flashed again. So the two friends met in the center of the grove, and Barnaby shook Corky's small pink hand delicately in his enormous talons.

So Corky staggered back to Bloquehedd Hall burdened with a dozen dragon skins of varied ripeness and received a welcome worthy of St. George himself and assurances of university preferences and certainly a shot at the pros.

And Barnaby returned to camp with Corky's sword and shield and a story which made the struggle to win them more epic than Armageddon. None of the young dragons even remembered their laughter at Barnaby's shame the day before.

Ah, but the scarlet skin of the fair Jessica pulsed like the embers of an unquenchable fire. "Yes," she purred. "From now on, maidenly and hard-to-get. Sooner or later," she smiled.

And of course, in the end, she was right.

"One of them" is an enemy fashioned from lies:
Poppycock propaganda, at bottom.
So it's wise to apprise unknown enemies' eyes
'Ere you gouge, gore, gun down, or garrote 'em.

BEAUTY AND BRAINS
ARE HALFWAY THERE

nce upon a time, long, long ago, when one's face and form were one's fortune, there was this queen named Tasmin who gave birth to a boy so ugly those in attendance fainted dead away, except for the hardy midwife, Helga, who had seen them all. This child, however, whom his parents had decided to name Honoré, was surely one of the most piteous Berta had ever seen. His poor little body was twisted and misshapen, one shoulder humped like a turtleback; his legs were bandied and destined to limp, and his great liquid eyes tended to squint around a sweet-potato nose.

"Ah, now, little queen," crooned Berta—who was also a bit of a sorceress, "this crookedy little lad will have a twisty body to be sure, but a loving heart as solicitous as a saint's. And intelligence? Ach, this boy will be the smartest since Socrates sat on his stone passing out learning like bread. That's your lad! He'll be able to give wits to a warthog. You just love the lad, *Liebschen,* and watch. He'll have a beauty all his own that none can take from him."

Honoré grew like a stunted shrub, galumphing about in the wake of the healthier children, laughing with them when they laughed at him. But gradually the children grew to take him for granted, like an ugly old dog in the family for years. Both boys and girls defended him fiercely when strangers baited the boy, and in return Honoré spun them tales that transported them all to lands of spicy and golden adventure.

Even as a toddler he showed knowledge beyond his years. He spoke complex sentences before he was weaned, learned Latin before he could walk, and polished off spherical geometry before his peers could read. He began adjudicating disputes among the children, always sensitive to the hurt feelings and bruised egos on either side and always rendering decisions that made each side believe it had won. But gradually he began advising the servants, and when news of his impartiality and empathy reached his father, the royal advisors began to seek his opinions, too.

Meanwhile, as Honoré was becoming an adult without becoming a grown-up, far off in a palace two or three kingdoms away, Queen Isabella gave birth to twin girls, Estella and Citronella, with the help of the peripatetic midwife, Berta. "Ach," sighed Berta as she put Estella in her mother's arms, "this child will be more breathtakingly beautiful than a peacock. And just as breathtakingly dumb." At which Queen Isabella winced slightly.

"And this lass," Berta said, putting little Citronella next to her sister, "will be as ugly as a plowshare. And just as sharp and tough." At which Queen Isabella groaned audibly. "Isn't there some spell you can cast, Berta," the Queen moaned, "that would even things out a bit more fairly? After all, sort-of pretty and sort-of smart are more the common thing. You would, uh, of course be handsomely rewarded." But Berta shook her head. "No, *Liebschen,* fairness is not the way of the world. And wouldn't it be a dull one if it were?"

So as Estella and Citronella grew, their good qualities increased geometrically. As did, alas, their less desirable endowments. Estella became more radiant than dawn, day by day; her skin was creamy satin, her eyes sparkled amethyst, and ambassadors from all over the world arrived to get in bids for their princelings before the child was five. Unfortunately the poor girl began to trip over her shoelaces from the first moment they were put on; anything breakable in the castle had to be put on higher and higher shelves each year that she grew; and even after she had entered her teens, she was not allowed out without the address of the palace on a placard tied around her porcelain neck. Truth to tell, what was within was porcelain, too.

Citronella, on the contrary, grew more physically repulsive by the minute; her skin parched and pocky, her hair like iron shavings, her figure like a lump of dough forever rising, and many of her ladies-in-waiting refused to attend her unveiled. Yet even as an infant she had an instinct for which sides the silver went on; and by five she had mastered Greek and differential calculus and had a rapier mind and whiplash wit that delighted all the court.

Now if you are thinking the perfect solution would be for Citronella to meet Honoré, remember that perfect solutions occur in other galaxies.

Whereas in their infancy, Estella had been the darling and Citronella the laughingstock, within very few years their roles—as they are wont to be—did a *volte face*. Young Estella would dearly have loved to surrender all her beauty and all the stares from young men who had only recently met her, just in order to make her limbs obey her will and possess an attention span somewhat broader than a meridian of longitude.

One day as Estella moped along a woodland path bewailing her rejection and dejection, she was startled to see a dwarfish young man sitting on a milestone. One shoulder humped like a turtleback, and his large sad eyes squinted around a sweet-potato nose.

"Beautiful lady," he said, jumping to his crooked feet. "So lovely yet so sad. Has some suitor brought this gloom on you?"

"No, sir," Estella sniffed. "No suitor. Fate."

"Forgive me, my lady. My name is Honoré," he said, bowing as deeply as he was able. "At your service. But you seem endowed with every favor fate could give. What has fate denied?"

"A brain larger than a mustard seed would help. Oh, dear!" she wailed, and Honoré sat her on the stone. "I'd rather look as appalling as you do if only I had a flicker of intelligence. *Oh!* Oh, *dear!* I'm *sorry!* I didn't mean . . . You see? I do that all the time. Oh, *why* must I be so clumsy and stupid?"

Honoré squatted next to her and looked up into her lovely eyes. "A great Greek once said a very wise thing. Only fools believe themselves wise, and only the wise know they are fools. No greater proof of wisdom than to believe you haven't any."

"Huh?" Estella squinted. "Oh. Uh. That's very . . . *deep*."

"I can put an end to your grief," Honoré said.

"But I've been to specialists," Estella moaned.

"There, there. I did nothing to deserve it, but in compensation for the body I bear, I was given the power to give intelligence to anyone I love. And, my lady, if you will forgive my boldness, you have stolen my heart from my crooked breast."

"I've done that often," she sniffed. "After an hour or so, you'll want it refunded."

"If you will promise to marry me within a year, I will give you intelligence from this very moment. You'll have a year to make up your mind. A trial basis. You'll find intelligence is not an unmixed blessing. And you may prefer to give up your quick-wittedness than marry me."

Well, Estella was a girl who couldn't extend her mind even to the next minute, let alone a whole year, so she leaped at the chance. In a flash, she and Honoré were discussing the music of the spheres, and the difference between the speeds of sound and light, and the relative merits of books Estella had never even read! Then she bade the dwarfish young man goodbye and tripped blissfully to the palace, scarcely able to contain her joy.

Overnight the palace was abuzz with the news: Stumblebunny has had a brain transplant! Estella sailed through the palace museum without breaking a single artefact; she danced the minuet with the grace of a swan; she delivered herself of witticisms which immediately became the talk of the palace, the town, the continent. Her father sought her advice on the most convoluted questions, and she became a valued member of the Cabinet. Her sister, Citronella, as one might imagine, was not one bit amused.

News of this dazzling beauty with the appearance of Aphrodite and the sagacity of Solomon began to spread all over the world, and eager princes came to seek her hand—especially those less mentally gifted, quite willing to exchange royal power for a wife with a mind like a razor and a body like mortal sin. They pressed their suits relentlessly, but she simply couldn't choose. Though she couldn't remember where she'd heard it—she remembered something from a life of which she had become amnesiac: "You'll find intelligence is not an unmixed blessing." And truer words were never spoken. The more one has, the more difficult to make a choice. The less you know, the more certain you can be.

Dithering over her choice of princes, whose assets and liabilities she had already listed on foolscap paper, two columns each, Estella had some vague sense that a walk in the woods might calm her nerves. As she strolled through the forest, trying to short-circuit her calculations, she came upon a bustle of servants setting up tables, putting pots to boil, frosting fantastic cakes. "What are you doing?" she asked a woman with sleeves rolled high and cheeks like raspberry puddings. "Ah, my lady," she said, "the prince. Tomorrow is his *wedding!*"

A memory was beginning to flicker in the embers of her mind.

Just then she saw him, his body parts as eccentric as a French curve. He was gussied up in a brocade doublet and silken hose, a feathered cap upon his misshapen head. "Well, my lady," Honoré said and gave her his rickety bow, "what do you think? I hope it's not too pretentious, is it?"

Estella murmured, "No."

"Well," Honoré grinned. "I've kept my part of our bargain. How was your year of intelligence? Bit taxing, I suspect."

"Yes. Quite."

"And today is the day of decision, is it not?"

"Well," Estella hesitated, "I . . . I haven't quite made up my mind. You realize, of course, that when I agreed to your proposal, I was a fool. And fools tend to answer quickly. Without proper pondering. Since you're very intelligent yourself, I have no doubt you are willing to listen to reason. To pause. To evaluate. Perhaps it would be better to go back to being stupid. I broke a lot of things, but I can't recall breaking any hearts. At the moment, the palace vestibule is strewn with broken hearts. You made a big mistake taking away my stupidity."

"No," Honoré said quietly. "No."

"You can't justly be offended," she said, "by a promise made by what was, in fact, another woman. A fool. I mean . . ."

"You argue deftly," Honoré said, with a sad smile.

"I mean, how could an intelligent man be angry at a breach of promise when he . . . when he sees it in the total perspective?"

"Perhaps, then," Honoré said quietly, "a promise is made not only with the mind but also with the heart. Not merely for gain to oneself—as the foolish Estella might have done—but also with a sense of one's honor committed to another."

"I would rather talk of justice," she said.

"Yes," Honoré replied. "Most would."

"But . . ."

"If a fool," he said, "could be hurt by a breach of promise, why wouldn't an intelligent person be? Should intelligence place one at a greater disadvantage than stupidity?"

Estella paused and pondered.

"Think," Honoré pleaded. "With the exception of my ugliness, is there anything about me that displeases you? My concern, my care, my intelligence, manners, character?"

"No," she said quietly.

"Then which do you reject when you reject my proposal? My body? Or my self?"

For a long time, Estella became very, very silent. Something was a-borning in her, beyond beauty or intelligence.

Finally, Honoré said in a very quiet voice, "You have the power to make me the most pleasing of men."

"How?"

"If you love me enough to *wish* it could be. You have the power to make me handsome."

For a long time more, Estella was silent. At last she said, "You have been so kind to me."

Honoré bowed his head and waited.

"Honoré," Estella said. "I wish with all my heart that I could make a choice that would set you free."

"And set you free, too," Honoré whispered.

"I do love you, Honoré."

In a flash, Honoré was transfigured! Tall, straight, handsome, strapping. Glowing.

When the two lovers returned to her parents' castle, the servants looked at them in awe. This ravishing bright girl capering at the side of a monster! But to Estella, what had been Honoré's hunched shoulder was little more than a shrug. His limp no more than a slight, bewitching sway. His squint a wink of delight from one with whom she shared the deepest secret of all.

There are arrant fools who believe the vault
Between lovely and loathsome uncrossable.
But the heart is a hunter not ready to halt
When informed that the quest is impossible.

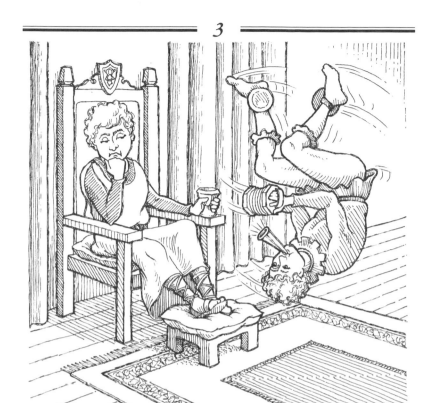

A FISTFUL OF STARS

nce upon a time, long, long ago, when living by the book was proof of virtue, there lived this prince named Eric, who was—to be candid—a stiff. He walked as if his parents had bound him to an ironing board; he always handed in schoolwork a day early; what's more he bathed— daily, without being told to, even though everyone else smelled like horse blankets. And he never laughed. Never danced. Never sang. "Frivolous," he sniffed.

His father, King Clement, was worried about the boy, and so he enlisted the help of Eric's squire, a gladsome lad named Will, to try to get Prince Eric to kick up his heels a bit, get into a few dust-ups, break a few things—

provided they were inexpensive. But when Will tried to teach him to dance, young Eric pursed his mouth like a testy child, folded his arms, and moved like a giraffe on stilts. When Will sang, Eric covered his face with a handkerchief. Will did pratfalls, cartwheels, backflips. Not a chuckle. He tried bawdy ballads, lecherous limericks, tales of illicit love. When he finished, he found Prince Eric had been reading the stock market reports. "You're a fine fellow, Will," the Prince yawned, "but sometime one must simply grow *up*."

King Clement had another idea. He would set Prince Eric to pass judgments in a minor claims court and set Will at his shoulder to suggest solutions both just and compassionate.

Well, the first case was a pair of women in dispute over a rooster. Dora was plump; Flora was thin as bamboo and looked like she chewed styptic pencils. Flora held the rooster. "Your Grace," dumpy Dora said, "we each had a rooster, but hers died, and in the night she put her dead Tom in my yard and took my Chanticleer. See, the bit of gold around his lovely eyes?" The Prince turned grimly to Flora, who was having difficulty calming the bird. "Nonsense," she rasped. "This is my Tom. That fat sack of doorknobs is driving the poor fellow wild." Will leaned to the Prince's ear. "Try what Solomon did. Offer to cut it in half." Eric scowled. "The woman is right. Possession is nine-tenths of the law. Next!"

The second case was a pair of landowners named Godwin and Godfrey. It seems a stream flowed through Godwin's land, then into Godfrey's, but Godwin had built a dam to make a pond where his geese could swim, so nothing but a trickle went through into Godfrey's pasture, and his sheep's tongues were lolling into the dust. Will whispered, "Godwin's pond needn't be so deep.

Geese have a shallow draft. Let him keep his pond but lower his dam, and both can be satisfied." Prince Eric glowered. "The dam is on Godwin's land. Possession is nine-tenths of the law. Next!"

The third case was a young wife who claimed her wretched old husband worked her harder than his oxen, complained about her cooking, and he beat her. Will leaned to the Prince's ear: "He has a reputation, Your Grace. This is his seventh wife. Each of the previous turned up their heels in exhaustion." Eric cocked a skeptical eye at Will's exaggerations. "Were you married properly?" he asked, and when she nodded, he said, "Then you said you would love, honor, and obey, did you not? You're the man's wife. Possession is nine-tenths of the law. Next!"

Fortunately there were no more cases, and the people began to pray ardently for long life for good King Clement. So one evening the King and Will sat depleting the royal wine cellars, trying to concoct a plan to lure Prince Eric into the human race. At last, after much retuning and refilling, they decided: Prince Eric would go on a quest, and not just any old quest, mind you, but a search for the fabled casket of pearls hidden some-where within the bowels of Mount Doom.

Ah, a fearsome place that Mount Doom! Many gallants had tried their fortunes there, but after awhile the sight of so many skeletons littering the paths quite emptied all bravado from the fortune hunters' souls. What was worse, legend had it the pearls could be discovered only at night and only during the most frighten-ing thunderstorm of the year. And the Royal Astronomy Academy, with unprecedented unanimity, agreed that the most frightening storm of the year would occur the very next night.

"Piffle," said Prince Eric. "Once one is soaked, one can't get any wetter, can one? And after we get within the caves, it won't be raining, will it?"

So off he rode in the gathering dark, with faithful Will following behind. Great rollers of thunder grumbled across the heavy sky, spikes of lightning spidering out from the black bellies of the clouds. Rain lashed the trees, and the trees in turn lashed the sodden riders as they passed. Then in a flash of lightning, Will cried, "Look, Your Grace! A cave!"

They scrabbled up over the rocks into the welcome black mouth, out of the rain. Will pulled pitch-coated torches from his saddle bags, and the two began to clamber over fallen rocks, deeper into the darkness. At last they came to a central chamber that echoed all round them and high up into the ceiling. Spikes of rock hung from the impenetrable dark above and dripped into pools, and up in that stone forest bats twittered and fluttered.

"This is *it,* Your Grace!" Will whispered. "I *know* it!"

"How?" scowled the Prince.

"Instinct, I guess."

"Fiddlesticks," the Prince sniffed.

But as they waded to the center of the chamber, there it was: A chest glittering in the light of their torches, mounded with perfect opalescent pearls!

Unfortunately, perched atop the glimmering chest was a bat about as large as your average condor. Her eyes were like ruby fists, and her hairy snout gaped and flashed stiletto teeth. And at the moment, as bats go, she did not appear overly welcoming.

"*Ha-aa-aagggh!*" she screeched, like a wet cork scraping glass. And "*Ha-aa-aagggh!*" she screeched again.

"Let me talk to her, Your Grace," Will said, shaking. "I know a bit of bat."

"What?"

"My grandfather taught me to talk to bats."

"This is one of your jokes," Eric said, not laughing at all.

"*Ha-aa-aagggh!*" Will screeched, and the bat's red eyes popped, for, though she was a world-class specimen, Will was considerably larger and louder than she. So Will began a cacophonous series of squeals and squawks that left both bat and Prince dumbfounded. In return, the bat—looking somewhat put-upon—set up a strident series of caterwauls herself, snarling and gnashing her considerable teeth in the bargain.

"Ah, that's it, then," Will said grimly.

"That's what, then?" the Prince said hesitantly.

"The tub of gold."

"What tub of gold?"

"It's in a cave, several levels down. She says she'll give up the pearls for the gold. She likes the light they make, not too strong. She has poor eyes, you know."

"Well, uh," said the Prince, having lost a touch of his starch after encountering the storm and the murky caves and the mother of all bats. "Uh . . . ?"

"Might as well get on with it, eh? Shall we go?"

So the two young men turned wearily to probe even further down into the darkness, following a thin, thin seam of gold in the rock which the bat had apparently pointed out to Will, though for a long time they seemed to be roaming in circles in a forest of stalactites. So, to keep up his spirits, Will began to whistle, and then he began to sing:

> "Shall I run and hide my fistful of stars,
> Or try to harvest them all?
> Shall I sit inside, secure by a hearth,
> When the sky's on fire with their call?
> Can a man abide the aching heart
> To catch them up where they fall?

Just to sit and be, makes a no one of me,
When the gods make the wind blow fair.
And it matters not if I find the spot,
In the going, I'm already there."

"Must you sing?" the prince inquired testily, nursing a knee he'd bashed against a rock.

"It lifts my heart, Your Grace."

"If only your head were as large as your heart," the Prince sniffed. "You've succeeded in getting us irretrievably lost."

"Ah, no, Your Grace. We'll do just fine."

"When a man *thinks,* Will, he tends not to be an optimist."

"Your optimist is your fool, Your Grace. But there's a long distance between optimism and hope." And suddenly Will stopped. "Well, now, see that, Your Grace?"

"See what? I can hardly see you."

"The seam runs out here. At the mouth of another cave."

So they crouched and stumbled into yet another cave, reeking with mildew and what the Prince suspected were decomposing things he'd prefer not to see up close. But as they came to the center, there it was: A tub of gold large enough for the annual bath of a family of ten. Unfortunately, coiled in the tub was a cobra who seemed also large enough to accommodate a family of ten.

"Ssss-*ssss-SSSS!*" said the cobra, as indignant as an archbishop caught in his bathtub.

"Ssss-*ssss-SSSS!*" said Will right back, bold as you please.

"You're not going to tell me you talk snake," Eric said.

"Not well," Will shrugged. "May be a different dialect."

The Prince rolled his eyes while Will segued into a series of hisses and splutters and sibilant wheezes that left the floor of the cave awash in saliva, especially once the cobra joined in, sizzing and whizzing and fizzing right back at him.

"Hm," said Will, when the sniffling and snorting had ceased and the cobra fanned his cowl around his fangs in indignation.

"Hm, what, Will?" Prince Eric wheezed wearily. "Not *another* swap. Oh, please. Not something in exchange for the gold."

"He likes the gold," Will said. "It's cool on his tummy."

"We could gather pebbles," the Prince said, ready to weep. "Nice, cool *pebbles,*" he said toward the snake, enunciating as clearly as he could. "It's the *latest* thing in the palace zoo. Really! Truly!" And the Prince giggled like a fool. When he saw his attempts to get on the cobra's good side were futile, he turned back to Will. "What does he want in exchange? And I suspect it's not in a cave just down the hall."

"The Scimitar of Solomon," Will said gravely. "Ever so big. Steel. Cooler than gold. And it melts less easily when King Cobra gets upset. See the golden puddles round his tummy."

And so they went, deeper and deeper into the rocky darkness, stumbling, clawing, probing ahead with their hands. And Will began to sing again.

"When I stand and feel the wash of the rain
Draw paths out over the sea,
Then my heart goes stealing out to attain
Horizons I've never seen.
Shall I turn my heel, a man in vain,
When gods are calling to me?"

And he began to sense Prince Eric humming along with him.

"Oh, the call may lie, but until I die
I must go when the wind blows fair.
And it matters not if I find the spot,
In the going, I'm already there."

"It does make the time pass, doesn't it?" said the Prince.

"Yes, Your Grace."

And on they plodded. Then suddenly they were in a cave larger than any they'd seen before. And in the center, suspended in an impossible shaft of light, the Scimitar of Solomon! As they stumbled toward it, both giggling with glee, they saw it was nearly as tall as a man, with a curved silver blade fretted with mysterious letters and a golden grip sparkling with diamonds.

Unfortunately, the shaft of light was a pillar of ice six feet thick.

The two young men sank exhausted at the base of the bright pillar, unable to speak from weariness.

"Well, we did try, didn't we, Will?" the Prince sighed.

"Yes, Your Grace. We did."

" 'In the going, I'm already there,' eh?"

But as they sat there, dozing, their torches leaned against the icy column, and a single crystal tear began to trickle down the side. Ever so slowly, ice chips began to slither down the shaft. Then there was a great crack! The two men's eyes shot open. As they watched, the sides gave way, and there stood the Scimitar of Solomon, ready to hand.

Unfortunately, through some mysterious vector of forces Prince Eric could have explained had his mind not been on more important factors, like staying alive, the column of ice had supported the cave's ceiling. Which began to crumble. And tumble. Across the doorway through which they had entered.

The two of them sat aghast, looking at the dust roiling across the sealed doorway. Then Will began to chuckle. And the Prince giggled. And soon the two of them were howling.

"Well," hooted the Prince, "it *can't* get any *worse!*"

"Careful, Your Grace," Will howled. "You're starting to sound like an optimist!"

"You know, Will," the Prince said, getting his breath, "if we ever do get out of here, the Scimitar is yours."

"But, Your Grace . . . what about the tub of gold pieces and the casket of pearls?"

"Be damned the gold and the pearls, Will," the Prince sighed. "My father has more than enough of those. You've given me so much more than that."

"I have, Your Grace?"

"Yes, Will. You've taught me to hope. You've taught me to sing. 'In the going . . .' "

Suddenly, they were terrified by a loud crash on the other side of the rockfall. They clung together, Will trying to catch a look at the Prince's face. It suddenly became serene. Then a broad grin stretched across Eric's young face.

"Of *course!*" he whispered.

"I'm sorry, Your Grace. When did you discover . . . ?"

"Just this moment, Will, When I learned to laugh. It was you and my father, wasn't it?"

"Yes, Your Grace. We . . ."

The boulders were falling away from them as the King's men pulled them from the cave opening.

"But how did you manage the bat?" the Prince asked. "And the cobra?"

"As you said, Your Grace, the Royal Zoo. After that it was mostly improvisation. Most of life is, I suppose."

"Ah, Will!" the Prince giggled, hugging his squire to him. "Ah, Will!"

*Oh, your proper and prim walk the cautious
    way
And prefer to make plans than face chance or
    romance.
Since the road won't comply, as the Irish say:
Don't give a sword or a crown to a man who
    can't dance.*

4

TAWDRY AUDREY

nce upon a time, long, long ago, somewhere between never and forever, there lived this king named Boleslaus who caught a bit of sniffles while out snaring snipe. More quickly than the court physicians could chart its course, the cold careened from head to chest and swiftly declined into *la grippe,* then tipped over into bronchitis, pleurisy, quinsy, and faster than electricity King Boleslaus had a one-way ticket to forever.

Now King Boleslaus left behind his wise widow, Magda, to act as regent until his only son, Schumann, was wise enough to reign—an eventuality of which even the kingdom's most dewy-eyed optimists despaired. Truth to tell, Schumann was a boy of monumentally modest talents and gullible as a goose. Thus, the king had bequeathed three others gifts such a limited lad would need to survive in a cruel and devious world: first, a ring to make the wearer beloved of everyone he met; second, a necklace which would enable him to accomplish whatever his heart desired; and third, a shabby old dropcloth which, however, had the power to transport anyone who sat on it to anywhere desired.

So Schumann slipped on his ring, his first bequest, and set himself to study assiduously so that some day, counter to the predictions of all the diviners, druids and developmental psychologists at the court, he would be a man to be reckoned with.

Despite a sweet simplicity bordering on the vacuous, Schumann made remarkable progress at the university. Although his tests ordinarily seemed retrieved from the bottom of a birdcage, his ring made him such an appealing student that his professors shamelessly pumped up his grades so they wouldn't have to see such a lovely lad sad. Not to mention the remote possibility he might at some time become their sovereign.

One fine day as Schumann was returning to the palace from classes, he chanced upon a ravishing young woman examining peaches in the market. Schumann stopped short as in a trance. Her hair was like spun amber, her face as flushed and tawny as the peach she held in her perfect hand, and her body the sort of miracle of which his tutors had warned him more than once.

"Good day, miss," Schumann choked. "I see you're . . . uh . . . inspecting the peaches."

"Why, yes I am, sir," the lady said, and her eyes drifted languidly from Schumann's head to his toes, examining the rich stuff of his clothes like a pawnbroker assessing a hock—which made Schumann so dizzy he thought he would swoon.

"My-my-my name is Schu-Schu-Schumann," the boy blustered.

"Ah, Herr Schuschuschumann," the lady smiled, "and I am Lady Audrey." And she held out her hand, which Schumann managed finally to kiss like a woodpecker goring for grubs.

"My maid this morning procured me the sweetest of cream," Lady Audrey said sadly, "and these peaches still have the glow of the summer in their cheeks. But . . ."

"Yes," Schumann stammered, unable to breathe.

"I am alone in this cruel world. I had thought perhaps to share my peaches with my maid. *Noblesse oblige,* you know. But I would so much rather share my peaches with someone of my own rank. Someone with whom I could discuss current affairs. Share the current novels. Critique?" Her ferny lashes fluttered.

Well, as things turned out, Schumann returned to Lady Audrey's mansion to share her peaches. And cream. And fascinating insights. And . . . well, no need for further details.

Several weeks later, still reeling from the rapture of his dalliance, Schumann lay with his head on Lady Audrey's lap, hardly able to believe his magic ring could have made his epically unappealing self an object of joy to so rare a flower.

"La," Audrey cooed, "*love*ly ring. Wherever did you get it?"

"From my father," Schumann said, not wanting to prejudice the lady's opinion against him because of his royal connections. "It's magic, you see. It renders anyone who wears it lovable."

"Oooh," she cooed again, "what a *precious* treasure for someone in . . . business. You must be ever so *brave* to wear it!"

"What?" Schumann inquired.

"To wear such a valuable ring in the *streets!* They're aswarm with ruffians and cutpurses. They could lop off your precious, precious finger just to procure it."

"I never thought of that," Schumann said.

"Well, of course, you *wouldn't,* would you, being so brave, and strong, and *manly?*"

"Well, actually . . ."

"I don't know how I shall sleep this night, knowing you walk the streets practically *begging* makers of mayhem to molest you."

"Well, I, uh, wouldn't want that. I mean, your not being able to sleep, I mean."

"Dearest, let me put it in safekeeping. No need for someone as desolatingly attractive as you to wear such a talisman."

So, Schumann left the ring with Lady Audrey, and so blinded was he by love that he quickly forgot he had once even had it. Until it dawned on him his grades were beginning to ease downward, then career, and finally plummet dizzyingly. He began to hear his professors referring to him in whispers as "Boeotian blockhead," "Cretinous chowderbrain," "Thundering dunderhead," along with other aspersions he was not quite able to decipher.

Racked with sobs and shame, Audrey threw herself on her divan, confessing her house had been ransacked by brigands, and his ring was forever lost. She even— not to minimize his loss—offered to commit suicide to atone for any part she might have had in this tragedy. Schumann, of course, demurred but returned dolefully to apprise his mother of his plight.

The Queen Mother tutted awhile about his gullibility, but she gave Schumann the necklace which rendered him able to accomplish his dearest heart's desire. As a result, his grades once gain began their climb, just in time for mid-year examinations.

Whom should our hero meet once more as he returned home with a report card with more A's than "The

Aardvark of Addis Ababa" but the lovely and lubricious Lady Audrey. At first she averted her sapphire eyes, lest he think her bold, but Schumann's gentle heart conceded that even temples were robbed once in awhile. So one thing led to another. Audrey invited Schumann to her home, where she granted his dearest heart's desire, and then some.

Schumann showered his beloved with perfumes from Araby, jewels from Ophir, damask and silks made by hands of elves and fairies. His gifts cost little since, mesmerized by the necklace, merchants fell to their knees and pleaded with him to take the goods off their hands for mere coppers. Finally, there was nothing else Schumann had to offer to evidence his bewitchment. Nothing, that is, except the necklace.

Audrey pleaded with him not to surrender such a precious gift, but Schumann insisted. Reluctantly, she accepted and said she would be his alone—after a journey to inform her parents in a land far, far away. A place called Ultima Thule.

So anesthetized was Schumann by dreams of his lady-love far away that he hardly realized his grades were again beginning to slump and merchants slammed doors in his face with oaths and cries of "Deceiver," "Mountebank," "Charlatan," and other manifestly untrue epithets. And after six months, fair Audrey had failed to reappear. That Ultima Thule must be *very* far away.

Schumann's mother was at her wits' end. "She deceived you *twice!*" she moaned, shredding a handkerchief reputed to have belonged to Helen of Troy. "Only one bequest left: the magic dropcloth. If you lose that, no sense coming back to me."

The next day, on the way to fail his final examination, Schumann happened to see none other than Lady Audrey bedecked more sumptuously than an Infant of Prague.

"Ah, love," Schumann cried. "I have such a *treat* for you!"

Audrey looked at him as she might at a tenacious tinker.

"Ah, my beloved, let me whisk you off to Samarkand!"

The lady's frost began to thaw. "Samarkand?" she said, not without some interest.

"Yes," Schumann said, bending over and spreading the cloth on the sidewalk.

"Whatever are you doing?"

"Preparing our transportation. Come sit down with me."

"Surely you jest. That unsightly . . . I should soil my clothing. It's filthy."

"Ah, but you've known me to produce magic before, no?"

"Well," she hesitated, sensing profit. "Perhaps . . ."

So Audrey sat next to Schumann, who clenched his eyes mightily and thought of the most blasted wilderness he could imagine, a barren waste denuded of bushes, howling with wild beasts, and crawling with vermin. Ultima Thule.

Quicker than thought, he opened his eyes, and there they were, in a no man's land stretching out to a craggy and lifeless horizon over which impenetrable darkness was beginning to settle.

"Oh!" Lady Audrey screamed. "What have you done? We'll be devoured by monsters! You have deceived me!"

"I learn slowly, I suppose. But I had excellent tutelage. Doesn't this look familiar? It's Ultima Thule."

The wrangling and remonstrations and recriminations began, and finally, exhausted by terror and tears, Lady Audrey guaranteed that, on their return, she would restore his precious ring and necklace, and wearied, the two fell asleep.

But as soon as she heard Schumann's heavy snoring, Audrey awoke and carefully, inch by inch, pulled the cloth out from under him until she sat on it alone.

Except for a tiny crowned serpent caught in the folds of her gown. She closed her eyes and wished herself back in the capital, and in a blink, she was gone.

Next morning, Schumann woke stiff and thirsty and looked around. Suddenly, he realized what had happened. Again.

All day long he trudged through the moonscape of rock and sand until finally he came to a stream. It smelled noxious, but his thirst was devastating, and he plunged his hand in to scoop out a drink. Pain rocketed up his arm, and when he looked down, the flesh had withered to the bone. Hours later he awoke and began to stumble onward, his stomach howling with hunger. He stopped at a tree arching down its fruit to him. He bit into the fruit eagerly and slaked his hunger and thirst, but to his amazement he found his body covered with carbuncles, cankers, and sores. "Ah," he sighed to no one in particular, "that's life."

"So it is," a voice said. Schumann looked down to see a dwarfed face clotted with knobs and nubs. "You don't look too peachy either, friend."

"Don't even mention peaches," Schumann moaned. "It all started with peaches."

"Well," the dwarf said, "life has been unkind to me, too." So he took poor Schumann to a stream where he bathed his face and instantly the flesh of his hand and body was restored.

"That was really *keen,*" Schumann said. "Thank you. Would you mind if I took a gourd of this miracle water with me? And a bit of the carbuncle fruit? If ever you're in the capital . . ."

Bearded from his long journey from Ultima Thule, Schumann entered the city to find a great clamor from the richest of the worthy burghers. The chief courtesan of the city, it seemed, had been afflicted by poison, perhaps from a snake intruded into her bedclothes by a jealous lover. Her name, it seemed, was Audrey.

"I," said Schumann, "am a great physician from far, far away. Perhaps I could be of service."

The worried merchants hustled him off to Audrey's house where he entered, disguised by his beard and oaken face.

"My dear," he said, "I can begin the healing process, but if there is anyone you've defrauded, you must restore the goods to your victims."

In fear of her life, Audrey confessed all and directed Schumann to a closet more chock-full of booty than the British Museum. He found his ring and necklace which he pocketed, along with a deal of treasure as interest, and turned to the once ravishing, now ravished, lady. "Eat of this delicious fruit," he said, "and you will find a way to be freed of your sins."

Schumann went home to his mother with his long tale and his three magic bequests restored. His mother and the fractious court advisors agreed Schumann had indeed finally found wisdom. So he was crowned king in unprecedented opulence and uproar. But King Schumann never forgot to be generous. Each day on his way to dispense both justice and mercy at the royal courthouse, he never failed to give generously to the hag who begged on the high street. Tawdry Audrey, they called her, a woman rumored to be atoning for her many sins.

But after a full year, King Schumann's heart was touched by the woman's patient endurance, and he sent his seneschal to her with the gourd of healing water. Audrey was restored and became—some say—abbess of a Buddhist convent in Ultima Thule.

This tale, we confess, skirts the edges of decorum,
But it has its roots in The Gesta Romanorum.
The gods as they assay our poor fates upon
*   their balances*
Show a certain predilection for the
*   singularly talentless.*

5

ENOUGH IS NEVER ENOUGH

nce upon a time, long, long ago, when things
had gotten about as bad as they possibly
could, there lived this worthy fisherman
named Zack, so poor that he and his waspish
wife, Prunella, were forced to make their abode in an
outhouse.

One day, sitting with his stout fishing rod at the far
end of the long jetty, Zack felt a huge tug on his line,
and he struggled to reel in whatever fate had sent. For
what seemed hours he labored, till his clothes were sodden with sweat and his old muscles screamed like a
man's on the rack. But finally he flushed a fabulous
flounder, six feet long, panting at his feet. "Well," Zack

said to himself. "This fellow will bring a fine price, and Prunella will not beat me about the head for a fool."

But the flounder's eyes flared. "Oh, Sir Fisherman," the flounder moaned. "I am no true flounder, but an enchanted prince. I speak not merely for my wretched self, but consider your guilt if I were sold and eaten. Slavery? Murder? *Cann*ibalism? It's unseemly. If not sinful."

Zack pondered a moment and realized the flounder had a point, so he eased the hook from the flounder's great jaw and carried him back to free him in the surf. The flounder surged away, leaving a streak of blood as he went.

When Zack returned to the outhouse, Prunella howled like a hyena in heat. *"Wha-a-a-t?"* she bawled and began belaboring him about the head and shoulders like a rug on a line. "You caught nothing *again!* So it's seaweed soup *again?"*

"Well, I did catch a huge flounder," Zack groaned, "but he said he was an enchanted prince, so I threw him back again."

The blows ceased, and Prunella backed away with a skeptical scowl. "You've gone balmy," she said.

"No. It's true. Ever so big."

"And you didn't ask for a boon?"

"Boon?"

"Boon, you ninny! Bounty! Reward! *Ransom!* You saved his life, you dimwit. That ought to be worth *something.*"

"It never crossed my mind."

"Well, let it cross your mind now, husband, or I'll crack the skull you carry it in! You get down there right now and whistle your enchanted prince back. Look at this stinking place. You tell that prince we want a cottage instead of an outhouse."

So, reluctantly, Zack crossed the beach and out onto the pier and called:

"Flounder, flounder, in the sea,
Come, I pray, and listen to me.
My wife, Prunella, will lay me low
Unless she has a bungalow."

The fish poked his snout out of the waves and said, "Bungalow?"

"Like a cottage," Zack said. "You see, right now we live in an outhouse. That's what most people use to . . ."

"I know," the flounder smiled.

"She says, well, I did save your life."

"Of course," the flounder said. "Go back. It's done. She has it already."

And when Zack went back, there sat Prunella smugly, in a little cottage with porch and parlor and pantry. Behind was a yard with hens and ducks, flowers and fruit trees, vegetables and vines. "Now that's more *like* it," Prunella preened.

"Ah," Zack sighed, "now we can live contented."

"We'll see," she said. And they had their supper and went to sleep.

For awhile, things were blissful in their little cottage, but after a week or two, Prunella's ebullience began to sag like a sunflower sensing a storm. Zack watched the tics and twitches in her cheeks, and he himself felt a thunderstorm brewing.

"All right, then," she said one day, jerking her great chin like a galleon entering a gale. "This house is too small, though it takes me forever to clean. With you squatting out there on the pier all day like a stump on a stoop. Go back and ask your flounder for a castle. And servants."

"Ah, wife," Zack sighed. "I wouldn't want to make him angry. And the cottage is lovely enough. What do we need with a castle? We wouldn't know how to act. And think of the taxes."

But Prunella began to batter him again. "You saved his life, you lily-livered lump! What could compare with that? If it hadn't been for you, he'd be making his way through some gourmet's guts at this very moment. Out with you. And don't forget the servants! And tax-free!"

So Zack shambled back to the pier and moaned to the sea:

> "Flounder, flounder, hear my plea!
> My wife, Prunella, will murder me.
> Save me, save me from that fate,
> For now she wants a great estate."

The flounder's face appeared above the swells. "Estate?"

"And servants."

"And I assume she's talking tapestries? Parquet floors? China and silver? Formal gardens? Coaches? The usual?"

"Well, I don't . . ."

"Go back," the flounder said. "It's done."

So Zack trudged back to the cottage and, lo!, in its place was an enormous marble mansion, with tall white columns and two staircases soaring up to the entrance. Inside, Prunella was sailing from room to room over the Oriental carpets, under the crystal chandeliers, running her calloused fingers over the ebony tables and chairs, barking contradictory orders to the servants.

"Yes," Prunella purred. "That's more *like* it!"

"It makes me nervous, wife. I don't know what to do with myself in such a great place. What will I say to the servants?"

"Shout '*Grovel*'!" she growled. "Then ask for anything."

"Well," Zack sighed. "No one could want more than this."

"We'll sleep on it," she said. And they did.

Next morning, Zack woke up in a bed the size of a stadium, softer than a sea of gossamer. Next to him, Prunella sat with her heavy arms crossed on her prodigious bosom. Her brows were knit over her knobby nose like two stags locking horns, and her mouth was pinched tighter than a skinflint's purse. Poor Zack realized that his helpmate had been doing some heavy thinking.

"You forgot the taxes," she growled. "We'll be back in the poorhouse before the year's out. And all our lovely things will have to go into hock. And it'll all trickle away into the king's pockets. I want to be the king."

"What!"

"Clean out your ears," she snapped and gave him a great jab in the ribs with her elephantine elbow. "Go to your fancy fish and tell him I must be king."

"But, wife, . . . how can a woman . . . ?"

In answer, Prunella raised a turnip-sized fist, and her face portended a resolve to rebuff all rebuttals.

So poor Zack shouldered into his shirt and donned his pants and plodded out of the cavernous chamber, along high-ceilinged corridors where portraits of ancestors he'd never known scowled down at him, down the curving marble staircase into the half-mile park, and off toward the beach. He sat on the old pier staring at the dark grey sea and mumbled to himself, "This is just not right. Just not right." But when he thought of what fate would befall him if he failed, he called in a tremulous voice:

"Flounder, flounder, hear my call.
Prunella's not content at all.
Behold the neck that she will wring
Unless somehow she's crowned the king."

The flounder rose from the waves and cocked a skeptical eye. "You're kidding," he said.

"I wish I were," Zack said, cringing.

"Does she know what being king involves?"

"I suspect not, but would that make a difference?"

"Very well. Go back. It's done. She's king."

So Zack went back, and just as he feared the flounder had been true to his word. The castle had mushroomed into a fortress with a broad moat and drawbridge, turrets and battlements. Sentinels beat kettledrums and blew ten-foot trumpets to herald the consort's return. Zack walked fearfully through rooms large enough to serve a circus, with velvet chairs and soaring ceilings. And there on a high golden throne crusted with diamonds sat Prunella with a great gold crown on her head and a jeweled scepter in her fist. Ladies-in-waiting in iridescent dresses sat on the steps like flowery garnish around a roasted pig. Dukes and duchesses scurried to and fro to do his biddy's bidding, and as Zack approached the throne, drums began thrumming so that he felt like a royal prisoner going to his own execution.

"Well, now," Her Majesty crooned. "That's more *like* it!"

Zack had no idea whether he should bow or curtsy or drop dead with shame. But he managed to stammer, "Well, this is as far as it goes, I suppose. We have just about anything any human being could ever dream of having. Now do you think . . . ?"

"Silence!" Her Majesty suggested.

"But surely . . ."

"Silence!" Her Majesty howled again from her great height.

"Oh, dear."

"There is *one* thing more," Prunella said, her eyes gone glassy and crafty like the glare of a gargoyle.

"Oh, my."

"I will be the *pope!*" Prunella thundered, her eyes blazing.

"You must be . . ."

"No!"

"But . . ."

"If he can make me king, he can make me pope. Go! Now! I will be pope before this day is out. Or *else!*"

Faint with fear, Zack shivered as he shambled from the palace. A great wind had risen, and clouds scudded the sky like angry warships. Trees whipped like demonic dervishes, and the sea tossed and pitched and boiled in fury. But weak with despair, Zack stumbled out onto the pier and cried:

> "Flounder, flounder, you won't believe me!
> I need your help. Oh, please relieve me!
> After all your magnificent gifts,
> Prunella's gone and scrambled her wits."

The flounder raised its nose from the waves. "I suppose now she wants to be pope."

"How did you guess?"

"A certain twisted logic to it. It's done. She's pope."

So Zack reeled home, and so it was. The fortress palace had ballooned into St. Peter's Square. Thousands with candles thronged the place, and through it all, perched on a high sedan chair and crowned with a tiara, came Popess Prunella, coped in gold and lofting blessings left and right. As she came toward Zack he heard her hiss between blessings: "That's more *like* it!"

"Pope!" Zack cried. "Excuse me. Pope?"

"Who," the popess snarled, "are *you?"*

"Your . . . ," his voice fell to a whisper, "your *hus*band. You remember. Zack?"

"Oh, yes. That will cause some canonical problems, as if we haven't stirred up a hornets' nest of them already."

"Well, you're at the top of the ladder now," Zack said, breathing a sigh of relief.

"Not quite," she snarled.

"But . . ."

"God! We can't order the sun and moon to shine. We can't turn the tides to our taste. We can't rattle the foundations of the earth and bring all sinners to their knees. Go!" she snapped and cocked her cobra's eyes in the direction of her guards.

Heartsick, Zack returned to the pier. The storm had turned into a hurricane, and trees were sailing through the air like unfinished canoes. Cottages careened overhead, and steeples speared after them. Thunder crashed and lightning crackled. And poor Zack stood trembling before the sea and cried, though he could not even hear his own words:

> "Flounder, flounder, don't reply!
> No one can ask this, even I.
> She's shot beyond all asininity.
> Now she yearns for the divinity."

The snout rose from the roaring waves, his great round flounder eyes flaring. "Nearly inevitable, wasn't it?" he said. "Goodbye, friend Zack. Go home now. It's done. You'll find Prunella where she rightfully belongs."

And when Zack returned, there was Prunella hulking unhappily in their outhouse.

We're made, my friends, of fickle stuff
For whom enough is not enough,
And forget in all our rude requests
In life itself we all are guests.

6

THE GRIFFIN AND FATHER FEATHER

nce upon a time, long, long ago, when fishes flew and forests walked, there was this tiny church over whose doorway was carved a most extraordinary griffin. It had a huge snarling sabre-toothed head, and from its scaly back rose great serrated wings, and its stout front legs ended in long talons. It had no hind legs, but the humped back tapered to a powerful tail coiled under the great wings and ending in a lethally barbed point.

A long distance from the little village dwelt the very Griffin himself, who had indeed been the model for the sculpture, though he himself was unaware of it until years later. One day a talkative magpie, too eager to tattle to be terrified of such a titanic fellow, tittered the news into his great leathern ear.

Now the Griffin had no idea how he looked, since he lived where there were no silent silver ponds, but in the mountainous wild where great cascades of water leaped suicidally from the crags and crashed in turbulent pools. So he determined to make his way to that village and make a long study of his lineaments. He leaped into the air and flew over the desolate wilds until he came late one day to the village where his likeness lay, but since the light grew dim, he landed in a green meadow to rest up for tomorrow's treat. His great wings were tired, for he hadn't flown that far in a century or more. And he lay his great tail into a cool stream since, when he tended to get overwrought, the tail heated up like an iron pillar.

Very early the following morning, farmers on their way to the fields happened on this heap of horror snorting softly in his sleep and scampered as fast as their legs could carry them back to the village with the unsettling news. Some old people suggested that the young men go out and kill the Griffin. The young men, not particularly stimulated by that suggestion, proposed they destroy the sculpture over the church doorway instead, obviating the Griffin's need to pay them a visit. But wiser heads realized that if they destroyed his image, the Griffin would be *really* upset, so the best idea was to do nothing and leave their fortunes to fate. So the people scurried into their homes like squirrels and locked their windows and doors, beside themselves with fear, since they knew how fickle fate could be.

When the Griffin woke, aching from yesterday's exertions, he spied two shepherds coming home from night watch, skewered them with his fiery eyes, and commanded them to halt. The two froze, immobile as fenceposts, except for the trembling and sweat.

"Don't you recognize me?" he rumbled.

"Ye-ye-ye-ye . . . ," which the Griffin took as an affirmative.

"Well, what's the matter with you all?" the Griffin growled. "A great many manlings have come by, but all they do is shriek and skedaddle. Isn't there anyone in your town who'll even talk to me? I'm told my likeness brings many visitors—not to mention trade—to your town. Bit ungrateful, I should say. Well?"

"Well . . . uh . . . well," the shepherds stammered, "Father Feather, the little priest who serves the church . . . He always takes the jobs nobody else wants."

"Then don't just stand there," the Griffin grumped. "Go get this Father Feather. Now!"

When the two shepherds arrived breathlessly at the church door, Father Feather was just emerging with three aged women who made up his usual weekday congregation. He was a kindly young man, eager to help and easy to dismiss. He conducted services each day, taught the unruly children, visited the sick, carried food to the poor, gladly helped people who found themselves in trouble and suddenly remembered a Father Feather even existed.

"Me?" said Father Feather. "But this Griffin has never heard of me. What should he want with *me?*"

The two shepherds were insistent, stressing the Griffin's displeasure at the delay and hardly able to control their imaginings of how many he'd gobble up if he were delayed further. So poor Father Feather, who cringed before a spitting cat, much less a highly irritated griffin, set off on his way, bent on deflecting any bane that might befall the town.

"Well," growled the Griffin when he saw the young priest approaching, "about time. I'm glad to see at least one person in that vile village with some character. Will you take me to this church which boasts my likeness over its door?"

So, knowing the people were all moled up in their homes and safe from any direct harm, Father Feather began to walk toward the village, the great Griffin hovering like a horrific iron kite over his head. Fields empty; streets silent as stone. When they came into the square, the Griffin looked up at the sculpture above the church door and settled with a sigh, gazing intently at his own image. He cocked his head first to one side, then to the other; he shut his left eye, then his right, squinting intently at every slightest detail.

"Handsome!" he snorted finally. "Quite handsome. I compliment the artist. That expansive forehead, those massive jaws!"

That evening, the Griffin bade Father Feather a fond farewell and said he would retire to his meadow and return next morning. When Father Feather averred that might not be in the best interests of the villagers, the Griffin scoffed. "I won't harm them," he huffed. "I eat only twice a year, first day of spring and first day of autumn. I find overeating makes me sluggish."

So day after day, the Griffin returned to admire his likeness, and gradually the villagers, reassured by Father Feather (whom they ignored in the best of times and trusted only in the worst), slowly began to emerge from their homes and go about their business, a tad unnerved by this great breathing hump in their square. But they more or less got used to him, as they might a meteor, dropped inopportunely but immovably into their town and with which they simply had to learn to live.

Yet each day some father sent his youngest son to listen to the big belly.

A few days later, when staring at himself from dawn to dusk began to pall upon the Griffin, he began following Father Feather on his daily rounds. First, the school where rowdy children were wont to treat their timid teacher with far less dignity than he deserved. Brazen boys dipped girls' pigtails into inkwells, and in reprisal the grim-faced girls cracked meter sticks over their suet heads. But when this great leathern dignity poked his sabred visage into the classroom, the children went stiff with shock, many instantly losing control of physical functions they had long taken for granted. Father Feather had no discipline problems that day, though he had some difficulty maintaining their attention, with such a mesmerizing visitor in attendance.

Later, the Griffin followed Father Feather on his rounds to bring food to the needy and medicine to the sick. To Father Feather's surprise, the Griffin suggested common herbs no one had ever considered healthful before, and soon many of those who had been ill were back to work again. And as the days went on, the Griffin found himself quite attached to the little priest.

But the villagers' nerves were abrading spiderweb thin. The first day of autumn was creeping closer, and who knew if the great devouring monster had an accurate internal calendar? If they could cage the great hulk, some suggested, he could prove an excellent tourist attraction. But some inquired, first, who could build a cage strong enough to hold such an epic ogre, and second, which of them was ready to invite the Griffin to step into it? So they finally met Father Feather and demanded he reason with the Griffin and invite him to take his presence elsewhere. Some suggested the little priest even lie, telling the beast there were far better likenesses elsewhere. But others argued this Griffin was no fool. Finally, one faction said, since the Griffin seemed to have taken a liking to Father Feather, following him about like a great scaly sheepdog, the simplest solution was to have the little priest walk out of town on an infinite trajectory into the wilderness. The Griffin would follow, and their problem would be solved. The proposal received almost unanimous approval, Father Feather being the only citizen with serious reservations about the plan.

But the poor priest thought and thought and finally saw it was, indeed, the only solution to save the town. So early next morning, he packed a leather bag with some bread and cheese and began his doleful journey out into the dreadful desert lands, willing to have the Griffin eat him rather than the children.

Only one hitch scuttled the scheme they'd hatched. The villagers suggested Father Feather had gone out in the wilderness to pray, for some time, maybe even a year, hoping the Griffin—who seemed quite irreligious—would follow. The Griffin expressed regret his friend was gone but showed no disposition to go after him. Nonetheless, he wandered the village disconsolate, realizing that staring at himself was once again not worth a full day's effort.

Then one day the Griffin happened past the empty schoolhouse. "Pity," he said to himself. "So much depended on this good man. I think I'll teach until my friend returns."

So he pulled the bell. A few children came running, sure one of their pals had pulled a prank. But when they saw the Griffin, their mouths lolled open. "Get the others," the Griffin growled. "In ten minutes, I'm coming after them."

Well, that schoolroom filled up quicker than a cistern in a flash flood. The great Griffin sat in the master's chair, his wide wings spread out and his sizzling tail lolling in front of the desk—except for instants when it flicked out to sting a boy whose attention had wandered. Within a few days, those children were learning as they had never learned before. The prospect of facing such a preceptor the following day made them sure they learned their nightly lessons as if their lives depended on it.

Then the Griffin began to visit the sick of the town as his friend had done. It was somewhat disconcerting having such a physician feel their pulses with his scaly talons and breathe sulphurously down their throats while inspecting their tongues. Near miraculous how many incurable malingerers regained their health.

Poverty simply ceased to exist. The Griffin cared tenderly for the aged—less moved by a kind heart than wanting to imitate the friend he admired—but no one was out of work anymore. All the able-bodied dragged themselves reluctantly to their neighbors to do odd jobs, which went against the grain but appeared far the lesser evil compared with a go-round with that gargoyle.

Summer had slipped away, and the villagers began to hear unexpected gurgles within the armored belly of the beast. Nearly time for his semi-annual gorge. The villagers began to fret for their children. Not to mention themselves. At a meeting, two elderly and unappetizing citizens were deputed to meet with the Griffin to offer a sumptuous meal of tenderest mutton, flakiest fish, most delightful desserts. Failing that, they were to mention an overcrowded orphanage in the next town. "Anything," they whimpered, "than have our dear children devoured."

"I wouldn't eat anything prepared by such cowardly, mean, and selfish people," the Griffin snorted in disgust. "Your very hands would poison it, if it weren't already. As for your snot-nosed brats, I've had enough experience of them to find them singularly unappetizing. The only brave, good, honest man in this village was Father Feather. I might have relished him."

"Oh, God," the old men cried. "Why did we send him away?"

"*What!*" roared the Griffin. And he forced them to tell him the tale of how they had sent their scapegoat out into the wilds.

The Griffin was furious. He rose on his wings and soared back and forth over the village, zoomed down on the terrified citizens till his tail was molten red. Finally, he settled in his meadow and lowered his tail into the stream, which hissed and sent up a cloud of steam seen two kingdoms away.

Finally, his rage more or less under control, he landed and rang the church bell. Trembling, the villagers filed in, more fearful of what would happen if they failed to appear than if they did. The Griffin paced before the altar, his wings trembling and his tail threatening to burn holes in the carpet.

"You contemptible wretches," he snarled. "Your Father Feather worked day and night for you ungrateful swine. As soon as you were in need, you were on his doorstep. Otherwise, you treated him more disdainfully than your dogs. Well, I am going out to find him and bring him back to you. And you will treat him as he deserves. You will bow to his goodness. You will serve him and honor him all the days that he lives. Or *else!*"

With that the Griffin strode through the quaking citizens. Outside the door, he turned and reached up his great rubbery arms and talons and wrenched his likeness from its moorings. Grasping it in his great paws, he leaped into the air and away he soared to the wilderness. When he finally arrived, panting with fatigue, he alighted and set the image above the yawning mouth of his cave—just as it had sat over the doorway of the church. And for awhile he lay studying his likeness with much satisfaction.

Then he rose again on his weary wings and went in search of the timid young priest. Finally he found him, half-dead, under the shadow of a rock. He picked him up in his scaly arms and flew back to his cave, ministering gently to him day after day.

When Father Feather awoke, the Griffin told him of what had happened after he had left the village and of what he had told the mean-spirited citizens: they were to treat Father Feather with respect, or the Griffin would rectify their unrighteousness. At that, Father Feather's kindly faced pinched in fear.

"Don't worry," the Griffin grinned. "A bluff. How you can love such loveless wretches defies explanation. But their fear of my coming will be as effective as my being there. And why should I stay among them now that my likeness is here to admire all day. Such noble features. Such magnificent proportions."

So he lifted Father Feather gently up and flew him back to the town, setting him down at the outskirts just at dawn. When the people saw him, they ran to him with nearly genuine joy, heaving him to their shoulders and carrying him in triumph to his church, heedless of the empty socket overhead where the Griffin had hulked. Better a timid priest than a tantrum-prone terror.

Each week the church filled to overflowing, and parents made sure their children knew their lessons on pain of punishment. Guilds formed to care for the aged and unwell, and men and boys doffed their caps and bowed low when Father Feather passed. For the first few years, they looked on him with dread, knowing what would

happen if they faltered. But gradually they began to see
how his kindness contrasted with their callousness, and
gradually they began to want to be like Father Feather.

We take for granted those who serve us
And quite forget they don't deserve us.
It often takes a winged surprise
To open our self-deadened eyes.

7

LOVE IS NOT A LOAN

nce upon a time, long, long ago, when power never played favorites, there was this Emir named Ahmed with three fine sons, Farouk, Feisal, and Fahd. Farouk, the eldest, was quite handsome, but weighed four hundred pounds. Feisal, the middle son, was also fine-featured, but weighed no more than a mosquito, soaking wet. Fahd, the last, had such a fine face and physique that maidens in the market stared at him and frequently fell into wells; yet he, too, was flawed: He was unshakably honest, which boded ill for his becoming a good emir.

Emir Ahmed also had an orphaned niece whom he raised as his own, Jasmine, whose beauty made lilacs leap, peonies pirouette, and mangoes tango. Slowly, the sons began to see Jasmine was not just one of the boys, but lovelier than light, and each was ready to commit patricide or fratricide, if such were her whim.

To avoid a family fracas more befitting barbarian Greeks, not to mention settling the succession, Emir Ahmed sought the advice of his vizier, Wazir, a crafty old man many presumed a wizard. At Wazir's advice, Ahmed proposed each son set out on a one-month journey. The Emir had a museum of eccentricities, so whichever son returned with the most interesting artefact would not only wed the heart-breaking Jasmine but gain his throne. Each was to dress as an ordinary merchant and allowed only thirty pieces of gold with which to trade.

The brothers vowed to meet at a tavern in the town of Haroun in one month and return to their father's court together.

On a long-suffering camel, fleshy Farouk found his way to Samarra where he poked and prodded all kinds of products, from greasy genie bottles to corroded magic lamps to ill-tempered claviers, but for the first few days found nothing. Then he encountered a one-armed merchant with the evil eye who offered a magic carpet to fly him anywhere he wished. When the wily chap lifted the scabrous thing from under the counter, Farouk pivoted his considerable girth and was about to depart. But the merchant insisted he take the rug for a trial spin, and with a skeptical scowl Farouk agreed. With epic groans he lowered his humungous hams onto the filthy rug, and with equally epic groans the rug managed to lift him up, up into the air, soaring over the city. When he finally skimmed to a stop outside the shop, Farouk willingly parted with his gold, got back on the rug and took off for Haroun, where he spent three pleasant weeks carousing with the locals while awaiting his less fortunate brothers.

Meanwhile, filament-thin Feisal found himself in fabled Bosra, where he, too, scrounged like a bag lady for three weeks through acres of junk till finally, about to give up, he was accosted by a one-armed beggar with the evil eye who offered him a way to see anything he wished, anywhere. Only thirty pieces of gold. He reached into his filthy sack and pulled out a rusty iron pipe, but Feisal scoffed and turned to go. But the beggar pleaded to give this wondrous pipe a try, so Feisal wished for a glimpse of the fair Jasmine as she was at the very moment. He put the filthy thing to his eye, and there she was, surrounded by her ladies, all about to enter the harem baths. Feisal could hardly take his eyes from this magic pipe. Eagerly he thrust the gold in the beggar's hands and began his trek back to Haroun.

Fahd had precisely the opposite problem from his brothers. Everything he picked up seemed a marvel, since he had been brought up in protective seclusion in the palace. He roamed the streets of Samarkand ready to buy objects commonplace to anyone else but miracles to him: waterwheels, butter churns, looms. But each time, his servant, a one-armed chap with a curious eye whom he had picked up along his way, tut-tutted and said there was better. Days slipped away, spent gaping at objects any child would ignore. Finally, he had only just time to get back. That day, his odd-eyed servant stopped at a stall and said, "Master. Here is your true wonder." And he handed him an apple. Fahd was feckless, but no fool. "There are apples aplenty in father's garden," he smiled tolerantly. But the old man assured Fahd this apple could cure any illness, known or unknown. Yielding, Fahd gave the old man all his gold to buy the apple and started back to Haroun to meet his brothers and return home.

When the brothers met, each brought out his treasure with smug assurance and looked at the others' with slight disdain.

"Hah," Feisal snorted at Farouk's threadbare rug, "Father wouldn't let his dogs do doodoo on that."

"Hah, yourself," Farouk snapped. "This is a flying carpet. I've tested it out."

"And given it a hernia, no doubt," Feisal sneered. "But look at what *I* found," and he pulled out his rusty pipe, at which even gentle Fahd snickered. "No, go ahead," Feisal said. "What would you like to see?" And he handed the pipe to Farouk.

"Delectable *Jasmine,*" Farouk drooled. He peered into the pipe, and his mouth gaped. "*Ah!* It is *she!* But . . ."

"What's wrong?" his brothers asked.

"Oh, my!" Farouk gasped. "She's on her bed, pale as death! Doctors all round her, wringing their hands. She is dying!"

The three brothers looked at one another in anguish.

"We must save her," Fahd said.

"But how?"

Fahd brought out his apple. "With this," he said. "It's a magic apple that can heal any illness, known or unknown."

"She's fading fast," Farouk said. "Quick. Onto my carpet. If it can carry me, it can carry a herd of elephants. Hurry!"

So the three boarded the carpet, wished themselves home, and faster than thought they were there. They rushed to Jasmine's rooms, and just as she took one last heroic heave of breath, they forced a piece of the apple through her liverish lips, and—in a blink!—she was restored.

But this remarkable recovery posed another perplexing problem. Each brother had contributed to it. Without Feisal's magic pipe, they would never have known Jasmine was ill. Without Farouk's magic rug, they would never have returned in time. And without Fahd's magic apple the ravishing Jasmine would now be a mere tragic memory. Which brother had, in fact, won?

A despot's duty is solving such dilemmas, usually through another test. Which is precisely what Ahmed suggested at Wazir's behest. Each son would fire an arrow in the royal lists, and the farthest arrow would cut the Gordian Knot, as it were.

Farouk shot well, if unimpressively. Feisal's arrow went beyond Farouk's. But Fahd's shot went beyond belief. In fact, no one could find the arrow. Which left Emir Ahmed in still a further fix. Technically, of course, Fahd had won the contest, the emirate, and fair Jasmine. However, no empirical evidence proved it. The arrow simply disappeared. But Feisal's arrow was there for all to see. Therefore, with a wisdom short of Solomonic, Emir Ahmed declared Feisal winner, and amid great jubilation, Feisal wed Jasmine and assumed the throne. Farouk, sure no other woman was worthy of him—or would have him, entered a monastery. But faithful Fahd went looking for his arrow.

After walking hours, he finally spied the shaft in a curious complex of rocks. No man could have shot so far. Some magic here. As he bent to pick up his arrow, he spied an iron door so cleverly crafted it seemed part of the rock. He wrenched the handle and it creaked open. Cautiously he moved down the steps, aware of light ahead. Gradually the corridor opened on a chamber richer than Fahd had ever seen. Icicle chandeliers cast a glow on fabulous tapestries. Liveried servants bowed as he passed. And at the heart of the salon sat a lady more lovely than music, smiling and holding out her hand. "Prince Fahd," she said, her voice a breeze through lilies, "I am Princess Primrose. Please. Sit with me."

Fahd sat, enthralled, delighted he had lost all those contests to win Jasmine, who now seemed a simpering schoolgirl. Then he noticed, hovering in the background, a one-armed old retainer with the evil eye, clad now in brocade.

"Yes," Princess Primrose blushed. "His name is Ali. Now you see my elaborate ruse to bring you to my realm. The carpet, the spyglass, the apple. And it was I who caused your arrow to fly out of sight, knowing your curiosity would bring you here at last. I hope . . . I hope you do not think me forward."

"Madame," Fahd said, his heart quivering, "I am your slave."

"Well, it was not precisely a desire to have you as my slave that impelled me to draw you here by such devious designs."

For days the two beguiled the time roaming the endless rooms, speaking of their lives, and opening their hearts to each other. Evenings, there were gala balls with elegant lords waltzing ladies like whirling bouquets and sumptuous tables laden with all manner of food. There were concerts, plays, ballets. And before a week was out, the prince and princess were hopelessly in love, and amid unsurpassed opulence they were wed.

Their marriage was rapturous, each moment convincing Fahd he could never stop loving Primrose, even if she were ever to stop loving him. But as the days wore on, Fahd began to worry that his father might believe he had left his realm in anger at losing Jasmine or perhaps believed him dead. So he asked his princess her leave to visit him, and trusting his love, she willingly consented, if only he not mention her hidden kingdom, located as it was within, but not a part of, his father's realm. Fahd agreed and set off for the Emir's palace with a retinue of twelve retainers clad in cloth of gold.

Emir Ahmed was overjoyed and called for a great celebration to proclaim his son alive again. But when the Emir pressed for details of his adventures, he was puzzled at how the young man, unable to lie, kept putting him off. Only a sweet smile and a promise to return. After three days, Fahd took leave. But once each month he visited, and each time Emir Ahmed's curiosity was further piqued.

So he took his puzzlement to his vizier, Wazir the Wizard.

"I'm puzzled, too, my lord," Wazir the Wizard wheezed. "Fahd and his entourage arrive ruddy and refreshed, not dusty and disheveled as after a long journey. Yet if he were in a nearby kingdom, we would surely have heard, no? And their clothes, eh? His servants' garments make your coronation robe look shabby. Where has he gotten money? Is it possible, out of jealousy over Jasmine, he has put himself into the hands of some hostile power eager to take over your realm and make him emir?"

Emir Ahmed truly loved Fahd. Really. He was sure Fahd meant him no harm. Well, reasonably sure. Perhaps slightly dubious. Scarcely skeptical. Nonetheless, he agreed the next time Prince Fahd visited, Wazir would follow him when he left.

The next month, when Fahd departed, Wazir the Vizier skulked after his party disguised as an old monk on a donkey, which took some doing, trying to trot after stallions. But he arrived just in time to see the last of Fahd's retainers disappear through the iron door, which clanged shut leaving not a trace of its existence. Wazir hightailed it back with the exciting news. Prince Fahd was under an enchanter's spell, for sure! Underground! In his own realm! The gods alone knew what vengeance the miscreant meant to visit on His Majesty!

"The next time Prince Fahd visits," Wazir the Wizard wailed, "have him flogged, flayed, and fried!"

"Oh, I couldn't do *that*," Emir Ahmed murmured.

"Then clap him in irons! Let him languish in the dungeons till doomsday!"

"Oh, there must be something less . . . decisive," Ahmed moaned.

"All right, then," Wazir the Wizard wailed, "at least a third test! Tell him to bring you . . . to bring you a man no taller than a tree stump, with a thirty-foot beard, who uses a five-hundred-pound iron bar as a walking staff! If he does, you can trust him. If not, he's a catspaw for some sorceress."

On Fahd's next visit, the Emir hesitantly admitted he had had him followed. He was a young man, as everyone knew, easily duped. Certain parties at court, he said, believed him under a spell. He offered Wazir's test, and Fahd went home disconsolate, fearing Primrose would resent being put to such a test.

But when he timidly told her his father's request, she smiled a radiant smile and said, "Nothing simpler, my love. Oh, Ali," she said and turned to the one-armed old man. "Would you summon my cousin, Akbar, for me, please?"

Ali raised his hand and, after several tries, snapped his kindling fingers, and there stood a man no more than two feet high with a beard that wound around his tiny torso and trailed behind him twenty feet. In his fist he carried a ten-foot bar that looked to Fahd to weigh at least five hundred pounds.

"Husband," Primrose said, "my cousin, Akbar. He missed our wedding due to some affair in Africa. He is a touch unmannerly at times, but I can entrust my spouse to you, can't I, Akbar?"

"Well," Akbar replied, his voice sounding like a gargoyle in a well, "if *you* ask, I suppose."

"Prince Fahd's father has put him to a test. He must have heard of you, and dared his son to find you."

"Rather unfatherly," Akbar growled.

"I fear he's been given bad advice," Fahd said.

"Well, what are we waiting for?"

So Fahd and Akbar made their way back to the palace, and as they approached the city, people fled like mice at the sight of this tiny man atop a great stallion, carrying an iron lance and dragging his beard a city block behind him.

When they entered the throne room, Emir Ahmed stood in awe at this uncanny mannikin, looking almost kingly with his iron mace and the beard dragging behind like an ermine train. And wily Wazir could hardly get his jaws to rejoin one another.

"Who is the one who gave this boy's father such bad advice?" Akbar demanded in a growl not to be gainsaid.

Emir Ahmed turned to the quaking Wazir, who croaked, "Oh, I, uh, suppose I offer a few suggestions now and then."

At that, Akbar raised his hefty staff and bonked Wazir right on his bald pate, at which the wizard's wan visage went white, and he withered away before their very eyes.

"Fathers should trust their sons," the tiny Akbar rumbled and turned on his tiny toes and trotted out the door.

And that was that.

No doubt the young need challenge
 to evolve,
A truth with which some folks become obsessed.
But one's child is not a problem one must solve.
Love worth the name does not require tests.

8

THE ART OF LOSING FACE

 nce upon a time, long, long ago, when privilege was not regarded as a privilege by the privileged, there lived this king with a daughter named Parthia, more lovely than birdsong at dawn. Suitors for her hand showed up at the palace more insistently than peripatetic peddlers. But after only a few moments in Princess Parthia's presence, each quickly withdrew, some even to monasteries, for Princess Parthia had a tongue in her otherwise flawless face more scathing than a scorpion's.

But as is quite often the case, the king was not getting any younger and needed to settle his mind once for all that Parthia would find a suitable consort, preferably one not too namby-pamby to administer a therapeutic thrashing at times. So he held a great banquet at which he had every available able-bodied bachelor for miles around lined up, in order of rank, from knights to barons to princes to grand dukes to kings. This was the princess's final chance. If she balked, the king secretly resolved to marry her off to the first chimney sweep who showed up at the gates.

Princess Parthia began her slow inspection up and down the lines, eying each contender from toes to top-knot as skeptically as a peasant poking pullets in a market. The first aging knight was quite red-faced from trying to pull in his paunch. "Sir Beer Barrel," Parthia sneered and passed along. And so it went for nearly an hour: "Lordling Longshanks," she snickered; "Duke Dump," "Earl Oily," "Viscount Vacuous," "Baronet Clarinet," "Prince Pockpuss," "Margrave Mealymouth," "King Cornshock," and so forth.

Finally, she came to King Conrad, a stocky man of middling years whose facelines bespoke a lived-in life, for he had been on two crusades as a boy, sheriff of his shire, chief champion of his father's realm before becoming king. "You have a mug like a map," Parthia tittered, "with every crag and path and goat track meticulously drawn! King Chartface!" And she turned to her fuming father. "What? No more?"

So the suitors departed, much relieved.

Then one day a few weeks later, a fiddler passed the palace playing for pennies for a piece of bread and a pint of ale. His hefty shoulder was hunched, his left eye squinted, and his white beard hung down to his knees. But his songs were so dulcet and his voice so silvery that downy doves were drawn by the sound and settled on his heavy shoulders. The king had him summoned to play for the court. When he had finished and was wiping the sweat from his craggy face, the king turned and smiled at Princess Parthia. "Wasn't that splendid, my dear?" he said.

"Excellent," she smiled. "As caterwauling fishmongers go."

"What is your name, fellow?" the king asked.

"Emery, may it please Your Worship," he said.

"Your songs have pleased us so well that I want to give you a reward. You may have my daughter to wife."

All the air vacuumed out of the chamber, what with all the courtiers gasping for air. Not the least unsettled was Princess Parthia, who was unable to make her lovely jaws articulate for some moments. And before she could utter a syllable, the priest was summoned and the deed was done.

So the grotesque fiddler took Parthia in hand and led her from the palace, through the town and into the woods, which was the longest journey she had taken on foot in her life. So far.

"What a lovely wood," she said, gasping for breath, not giving a weasel's whisker for the wood but wanting an excuse to sit down. "Whose wood is it?"

"King Conrad's," Emery growled. "The one you called King Chartface. It's gotten around, you know. Everyone calls him that. If you'd married him, this would all be yours. Up!"

As they dragged themselves onward, Parthia kept asking whose pastures were those and whose town is this, and always the answer was "King Chartface's." And each time, the girl set up a moan like a hound howling at the moon: "Ah, me!" she mourned, "If only I'd married King Chartface!" which, considering the number of manors and mines and millraces they passed, began to grate on Emery's nerves like a child chanting "Ninety-One Bottles of Beer on the Wall."

"It does not please me," he said through gritted teeth, "to hear you always wishing for another husband. You *have* one. You can have but one at a time."

Finally, they approached a tiny hut. "Goodness me!" Parthia fluttered. "We're not going to spend the night in this filthy hovel, are we? Surely there must be an inn."

"This is my house," Emery snickered. "And yours, my proud beauty. Till death do us part." And he humped in the doorway.

"But where are the servants?" she scowled.

In answer, Emery held a mirror to her face. Princess Parthia gasped, seeing her lovely hair all awry and her poor sunburned face, which she'd never known had a tendency to freckle, since she had never left the palace without a servant to shield her with a sunshade. "Are you mocking me, you lout?" she snapped. "Showing me how you've degraded me?"

"No. Just showing you the servants."

The days hauled themselves past, and poor hump-backed Emery found he had to do the work of two, since the king's daughter hadn't the slightest notion even how to light a fire, much less boil water. But after awhile they settled into a routine, and she began to understand that you had to gather kindling and strike the flint and haul the water and clean the grate. Yet it had disastrous effects on her alabaster fingers, which shriveled in the hot water like pale sardines. And each day she caught herself seeking out the mirror, like a cynical familiar, and each day it showed a young woman who would one day be as wrinkled and sere as King Chartface himself.

"We can't have you lolling about here all day," Emery said. "Earning nothing. We will set you to making baskets." So he brought home bundles of willows and reeds and showed her how it was done, and he retired to the shop in back where he turned pots on his wheel and baked earthenware in his oven. But the tough willows made her hands bleed, and she set up such a long-winded wailing that he tried to teach her to spin. But the hard thread cut her fingers, and she started caterwauling at the sight of the blood till Emery could stand it no more.

"All right, then," he said finally. "With a set of howler lungs like that you could make a hell of a huckster. We'll set you to selling my pots and earthenware in the town market."

"Oh, *no-o-o-o!*" she squealed and sniveled. "What if my friends from court should see? I'd simply die."

"Sell or starve," Emery said. Thus, Parthia trudged off behind her husband to the town which, to her disgrace, was not in King Conrad's domain but her father's.

At last Emery had found a task for which Parthia was fitted. All kinds of customers flocked to purchase her pots, since she was so delightful to look at. Some toothless old men paid her simply for the privilege of sitting with her and drooling. Most painful of all, many of her friends from the palace came with vinegar smiles and gave her money without taking the paltry pots, just for the sheer grim glee of watching her grovel. This, Parthia huffed, was too humiliating for words. To Emery it was positively peachy, for the pounds and pence were piling up.

Then one morning when Parthia had just set out her crockery in rows and ranks at the edge of the square, suddenly round the corner came a drunken hussar on horseback heading for home after a night's carouse. Right through her display. Bash! Smash! Crash! Chips and shards flew every which way! And when the debris had settled and Parthia could finally get her breath, she sat and surveyed the chaos round about her. Not even a single china chamberpot was left unshattered. And what would Emery say?

What Emery said was: "Only a numbskull would set up fragile pottery at a streetcorner where any passerby could boot them to Bedlam! You may be a princess, but you're not worth the price. All right! All right! Leave off the weeping and wailing and gnashing of teeth. We'll get you a job in the kitchen of the castle. At least you'll get our food for free."

And so Parthia found herself scrubbing crusty pots, scouring greasy floors, scraping messy platters, and none too proud to lick her fingers after. All day long, she'd stuff the leavings in her pockets, and she and Emery ate far better than before, since she didn't have to cook but only warm the food by the fire.

One evening there was a great ball, and Parthia was drawn upstairs helplessly to gape at the gaiety she once took for granted. The hall was a forest of fire, with candles blazing everywhere. Radiant ladies in satin and silks whirled in the arms of elegant gallants, and Parthia reached absentmindedly into passing platters, stuffing squabs and squirrels and squid in her patched pockets, her haughtiness humbled by hunger.

As Parthia stood there greedily drinking in the grandeur and laughter, swirling in place in her sweat-soaked shift, she felt a tap on her shoulder and turned to see a richly clad gentleman bowing her into a dance. But as he rose, her heart clutched in her chest, for it was none other than King Chartface, the suitor she'd so icily scorned. Her struggles to evade him were to no avail, and he swung her into a whirling waltz. Faster and faster the music mounted, and wilder and wilder they wound their way.

Heady and breathless at being back where she belonged, Parthia was unaware her pockets had ripped, and her whirlwind wake was strewn with pork chops and pigeons and potatoes she'd pilfered. Ere long the ballroom looked not unlike the floor of a butcher's shop or the village dump.

She was unaware, too, of the sudden silence, and then the titters, which turned to guffaws and erupted in bellylaughs. She broke from King Chartface's arms and pivoted slowly about, wretched and red-faced in the midst of the maddening mirth. Tears streaming down her face, she turned and hurried toward the stairs. But when she got there, a man stood with a violin under his chin and a long white false beard draped over his shoulder.

King Chartface.

He began to play, songs so dulcet and in a voice so silvery that downy doves were drawn by the sound and settled on his heavy shoulders.

"Yes," King Conrad smiled. "Your husband, Emery, sandpaper to your selfishness. Cruel kindness was my wedding gift to you. And I was the wild hussar who cracked all our crockery. The potter who turned a vase like you, no better than an ornament, into a rough-hewn pot of some simple use to someone."

Parthia's tears were hot on her cheeks. "I have done great wrong. I'm not worthy to be your wife. And look at me. No better than a slattern."

"Ah," said Conrad. "You were surely not worthy when we wed, but now we have shared our sorrows, we are worthy to be one. You are not a slattern, my love. Now you are fit to be queen."

So King Conrad had Parthia carried off by maidservants who bathed her and clothed her in silks and dressed her hair with diamonds. And when she returned, her father—who had been aware of the ruse all along—was there with all his retinue, and they cheered, and cheered, and cheered.

Some wear a face that is clearly satirical,
Like a place they might visit, but not their home.
Others have faces both lovely and lyrical,
But a fate-formed face is an epic poem.

9

A QUIXOTIC QUEST

nce upon a time, long, long ago, when the undeserving poor still believed hard work paid off, there was this boy named Leary, the son of a very poor carpenter. I mean, so poor that blind men smelled their unwashed bodies walking by and split the take of their tin cups. All day they toiled, but no sales. Who needed floors or doors, chairs or stairs, porches or torches? What they needed was food. And warmth. Most of the villagers had burned their wretched furniture all through the wrenching winter, ignorantly preferring life to creature comforts. But Leary and his father still worked, from well before dawn till well after dusk, if only to distract themselves from the hunger bellowing in their bellies.

Each night as they sat down to wood-shaving soup, Leary's father sighed, "Pray hard, Leary, and tomorrow will be better." Leary was beginning to grow skeptical, but his father was a loving man and knew more of life than he did. That night Leary prayed so hard he nearly imploded, but next morning, they found not only that their lot had not improved, but in fact, the villagers had stolen all their wares for firewood. And their fence and shingles. Even their outhouse.

"Pray hard, Leary," his father sighed, "and . . ."

"Hold it, Papa," Leary said, his patience worn thinner than the skin of frankfurter. "I'd like to have a word with this God, face to face. Where can I find him?"

"Why . . . in heaven," father gasped. "But it's far, far away."

"I'll find it," Leary snorted, and he tugged on his coat and scarf and mittens, and off he trudged into the dark, snow-silent forest. The trees loomed up like ermined mutants, all spindly arms and torsos wrapped in white. "God?" the cynical cypress sneered. "Fine chance." "God?" the laconic linden lisped. "Surely, you jest." "God?" the cackling chestnuts chorused. "Go back to the porridge on your plate. That's all you have. And after that, there's nothing."

Around noon, as Leary's toes felt stiff as stones, he pushed through the bushes and beheld a shimmering silk pavilion. Its rainbow sides tapered upward to golden pennons on silver spikes. And through the doorway oozed this very, very *dishy* lady. Her hair was molten gold, her face a Greek goddess's, and the rest of her was pretty Olympic-class as well.

"Hey, little bon-bon," she purred, "nice 'n cozy in here. And *lots* of food. And dandy drinks. And maybe a bitta after-lunch diversion?"

"*Wow!*" Leary cried, "You *betcha!*"

"One hitch, sweetcakes. Ya gotta become my slave."

Leary pondered that, and his tummy and toes and the tip of his nose offered pretty persuasive arguments in the lady's favor. After all, what the lady offered—dinner, drinks, and this seductive and perhaps instructive "diversion"—seemed at least at the moment more qualified to fulfill his needs than some quixotic quest. But something in this alluring lady did not remind Leary of his dear-departed Mum, so finally, he mumbled, "No, thank you," and trudged back into the snow-dense woods.

About supper time, the quest now seeming not only futile but quite likely suicidal, Leary came upon a wagon painted in bright curlicues and airy arabesques: "Doctor Fantastico! Consultant to Kings! Prestidigitator to Princes! Enlightener of the Unwashed! Palms Read While You Wait! All Wishes Fulfilled!" So he hauled himself up the hill and rapped on the tailgate, and a curious old fellow with white hedgerow eyebrows popped up.

"Ye-e-e-ess?" said the sage personage.

"I have a wish," Leary said.

"Don't we all. Any money?"

"Not a farthing, but . . . I'd do anything for some food."

"*Anything?*"

"Well, just about."

"Young fellow, I'll make you rich as Croesus and handsomer even than Wayne Newton."

"Wow! What do I gotta do?"

"Give me your soul."

"You're not serious."

"Never more."

Well, Leary's digestive juices made insistent pleas that a soul was, at least in the short run, a small price. On the other hand, a body without a soul would be dead, even if it was handsomer than Wayne Newton. On the *other* hand, live fast, die young, and have a pretty corpse. On the *other* hand, how could he sleep with himself without his self? On still the *other* hand, why were so many strangers interested in co-opting the soul of a boy? So Leary looked longingly at the lean loin lambchops and the escarole and the filet of sole the magus offered. A soul for a sole? It sounded better than it really was.

"No, thank you," he said and turned for home.

And of course he got completely lost. Wind keened through the roots of trees that hooked their barren feet into the turf. It whirred through their spindly hands, whirling in the empty sky and threatening to swoop on him. Snow snuffled under his collar and burned his skin. Where was home? Where was God? His weary limbs were telling him that the wisest idea was to crawl under the snow and sleep awhile.

Suddenly, as he stumbled through the drifts, he heard, nearby and yet far off: "Help! Anybody dere?"

Leary blundered toward the voice, pushing through the angry brush, and finally came to a big pit in a clearing. He peered over the lip, and down below was an old, old man with a gold front tooth. "Ah!" gasped the man. "You halp me?"

Leary got a long branch and, with a great deal of tugging and grunting, managed to haul the old man out, and both lay gasping at the foot of an old, old dead tree.

"Ho, you are goo' boy," the old man said. "Here," he said, "een my pawket. Fleent. You make us fire."

So Leary labored at the flint and tinder and finally started a fire. The two of them huddled in its warmth, and the old man tucked Leary under the flap of his big overcoat. "Ah," the old man said, "I am Manuel. Here, in awther pawket. Bread." And he broke a sodden clod of bread in half, and the two of them set to it, savoring every crumb.

"I'm Leary, the carpenter's son," the boy said. "Our prayers for food didn't work. So I set off to ask God about that. But I just got lost."

"Ah," Manuel giggled. "I work as carpenter awhile, too, as boy. Hm. You looking for God? Look up, *nino.*" Leary looked up at the sky, ablaze with a thousand thousand chips of crystal. "Now, smell de hair." And Leary filled his lungs with the crisp night, heavy with the tang of pine sharpened by the cold.

So Leary and Manuel sat and watched the stars and smelled the night, like praying, and slowly dozed off to sleep.

Next morning, Manuel was gone, and when Leary woke, his head rested against the corduroy flank of the old, old dead tree. He poked the fire to life and turned, wishing old Manuel had left him a bit of bread. To his astonishment, the old, old dead tree had sprung to life. Great green leaves lolled from its branches, and from their supple arms hung apples of solid gold. As the morning sun caught them, the tree seemed to catch fire, a bush ablaze, and from it came the voice of old Manuel: "Yo, leetle *nino!* You din 'spect me to do it *all,* hey? Dat's why I geeve brains, *nino.* Pray jawst for courage, eh? For to know you're not alone. Live well, my *nino.*"

So Leary picked a shirtful of golden apples and ran home, and all the villagers trooped out to celebrate—not to mention putting the arm on Leary for an apple or two. But since the tree had been a gift to him in the first place, Leary didn't mind at all.

The poorest among us is bountifully
 blessed, more
Than all of earth's creatures have been.
And often the answers we avidly quest for
Are closer to us than our skin.

10

THE GIGGLING GOAT

nce upon a time, long, long ago, when wishes still sometimes worked, there lived a hefty widow named Hedwig who was blessed with three daughters, Una, Trina, and Norma, all of whom spent their summers working with a traveling circus. Una was thus named as she had but one eye, smack dab in the middle of her forehead, which was much oohed-and-aahed over by peasants all over the land. Trina's name came from her thrilling three eyes, one smack dab in the middle of her forehead and two others more or less where everybody else's are, and Trina's three eyes provided even more *divertissement* for the downtrodden than did Una's one—a source of some strain on their sororal sweetness.

The one thing that kept the hellcat sisters from each other's throats was their mutual disdain for the third sister, Norma, thus named because she had the same sort of eyes as anyone else. So she swept the stables, watered the weird beasts, and was the only one the rumbustious roustabouts trusted to tally the take and sort out the salaries.

During the off seasons, when the circus was sabotaged by weather and the peasants' pennilessness, the three sisters and their sour-faced Mum lived in a cottage in the forest, where Norma did the daily chores and endured their dirty looks and catty critiques: "I swear you put *starch* in my undies," Una groaned; "There's not enough ice under my oysters," Trina trilled; and "What *good* are you, you silly slattern," Dame Hedwig howled, "with your ordinary eyes. Go tend the goat!"

As one might expect in this singular menage, even the goat, whose name was Helga, was a member of the circus. Jet black she was, with a single silver horn, which made her awesome to the great unwashed, believing she embodied evil. Actually, Helly was a sweet-tempered nannygoat, constantly giggling "Angh-angh-angh- *angh,* angh-angh-angh-*angh,*" like a hyena with hiccups, since she found the human scene so dreadfully droll.

Norma led the genial goat out onto the hillside and let her forage, and she sat at the foot of a tree and began to weep, her tummy gurgling, since she was given only the scraps her gifted sisters and miserable Mum foreswore.

"Why do you weep, little sister?" Helly the goat inquired.

"Oh, Helly, Helly, fill my belly. I'm faint for food," poor Norma cried.

"Nothing *sim*pler," Helly giggled, "angh-angh-angh-*angh!*" And hardly had she bleated the words than at Norma's knees a tablecloth billowed and spread itself, and on the cloth were silver salvers of salmon, platinum plates of plover, crusty croissants, and six different kinds of ice cream.

"Don't bother your head for the leftovers," Helly honked, "angh-angh-angh-*angh!* I'll take care of those."

Finally, when Norma sat back fit to burst, she said, "Helly, I think I'm full."

And with that the goat stepped to the meal and vacuumed the whole thing in, cloth and all.

In the evening, after she'd led Helly home, prepared the meal, and her family had troughed, she found that as usual they had scraped their leftovers onto an earthenware dish for her to eat. But she did not touch it. Next morning after she'd left to take Helly to the hill, the broken bits were still there. Day after day it was the same, and finally even her startlingly unbright sisters began to wonder. "Something abnormal with Norma," Una hissed. "Of *course* there is," Trina sneered, "she has only *two* eyes. Oh," she simpered, "I'm sorry, Una dear, I quite forgot." Una scowled but let it pass. "I'm going to get to the bottom of this," she snapped. "She's getting food from somewhere else. She'll start getting independent and snippy." So as Norma led Helly out to the hill, Una trailed behind.

But Norma spied her creeping through the goldenrod and gilley flowers and knew what was on her mind. So she set Helly into the bright meadow and trailed her toes in the stream. Una crept along the hill like a dog on a scent and propped herself against the hooves of a tree. As the morning warmed, Una's head began to sag, and her one eye fluttered, and she fell asleep.

"Helly, Helly, fill my belly," Norma whispered and, quick as a quark, there was her mid-morning meal. When she'd finished, she whispered, "Helly, I think I'm full." And in one caprine gasp little Helly sucked in the lot, cloth and all.

So when it came time for Norma to return home and prepare her mother's and sisters' meal, she shook Una by the shoulder and said, "Sister, it's time to go home."

Una shook herself, sure she'd been had, and grumbled to her feet. When they returned, she said to Trina, "Drat! I fell asleep! The minx is up to something. She put a spell on me!"

"Don't worry, dearest sister," Trina cooed. "I have three times as much ability to observe as you."

So next morning, Trina crept up the hill after Norma and Helly, nose to the ground like a serpent slithering through stinkweed. But Norma saw her shadow oozing along and went to her work, settling Helly on a hillock of clover and waited for Trina to doze in the sun. Trina's triple eyes fluttered awhile, then flickered, then fell.

"Helly, Helly, fill my belly," Norma whispered. And swift as a swallow, there was her meal. When she'd finished, she said, "Helly, I think I'm full," and whoosh! the meal was gone.

But Trina, who was a soupçon sharper than Una, often managed to sleep with only two eyes shut. And she saw the whole thing. When the meal appeared, it was all she could do to keep her two auxiliary eyes and her ample mouth from popping open. When it disappeared, she stole back to the cottage.

"*Well,*" she huffed to her open-mouthed mother and sister. "And what do you think of *that?*"

"And who does she think *she* is?" Una snorted.

"We'll see about *this,*" Hedwig hooted.

So they waited at the door till Norma came home. From far off she saw them standing there, arms crossed on their bolster bosoms, and Norma's surprise began to melt into fear. When she reached them, she saw a great butcher knife glinting in her mother's great paw. Fast as a flash, the knife shot out and slashed poor Helly's throat, and down she went, eyes fixed on forever and legs splayed out like a weather vane.

"Yes," Dame Hedwig purred. "I've had a hankering for roast goat all this day. Clean her up, *girl*. And have her ready by sundown. Come, girls. You must have your beauty rest."

So, tears streaming down her face, poor Norma dressed the goat and prepared her for what seemed a cannibal feast, silently lamenting her kindly friend, knowing life's blessings are brief, and seeing the lean days ahead once more. But she took Helly's kind heart and buried it by the cottage door, so she'd have at least some sad sense she was not alone.

Next morning when they awoke, to their astonishment a magnificent tree had sprung up at the side of their door, right where Norma had buried Helly's heart. Its leaves were silver sabers, and within them hung ruby apples.

The four gazed in awe. Then Dame Hedwig huffed, "Our circus days are done! Goodbye to the six-legged llama and the talking tiger and that dreadful Bearded Babette! High society, here we *come!* Una, climb up and pluck some of those wondrous apples!"

So Una shinnied up the trunk and edged out onto a limb. But when she reached for the ruby fruit, it kept slipping away like a sulky cat. Then the silver leaves began slashing at her wrists and arms. "Mo-*thurr!*" she cried.

"Oh, come down from there," Dame Hedwig huffed. "Trina, you get up there and try."

So Trina tried, but with the same results. So the mother sent up Norma. When Norma reached out, the glistening red fruit seemed to ease into her hands and even purr with delight. She plucked them and dropped them down till her mother and sisters had three aprons full of ruby apples.

The next few months were a flurry of shopping and spending. The two older sisters and their mother hired seamstresses from miles around to swath their considerable girths in garish gowns more suitable for the circus than society soirees. Dame Hedwig had a huge silken pavilion erected in the arbor and invited all the local gentry to attend a gala gathering. Cooks were engaged to concoct the most delicious dishes, and hired servants scurried to and fro setting up sumptuous tables, arranging flowers, chilling wine, and polishing silver. And of course, among them, poor Norma slaved like a kitchen scullion.

No one came.

So there they sat, three deflated hot-air balloons in florid frumpery, fanning their fiery faces and thinking foul thoughts. The servants idled in the arbor, and stableboys hired to hold the horses yawned, and the cooks began to whisper that in a day or two these mountains of food would be an environmental disaster.

Then down the path came a single rider. As he approached, they could see he was a knight, sheathed in silver chain mail on a chestnut charger. The servants stirred, and the stableboys stumbled to their feet, and the cooks began to chortle, sure that this was merely the first swallow of spring. The weird widow and her dumpling daughters rose and smoothed their dreadful dresses and pasted smarmy smiles across their faces, craning their necks and straining their numerous eyes beyond the knight to see the inevitable parade of guests of whom he was but the forerunner.

But he was alone.

The knight dismounted and bowed to these three buxom personages, biting back a grin at their garish getups and their impressive assortment of eyes. "My ladies," he said, "I am Sir Gareth. The King has heard of your magic tree and wonders if you might consent to part with a branch that he might plant in the castle garden. Of course, you would enjoy his undying gratitude. There is little he could deny you."

Hedwig eyed this handsome fellow, and one could almost see within her piggy eyes the calculations cooking. Here, she thought, was the pathway to acceptability.

"Would the gracious King be willing to marry one of my precious daughters?" she asked, her eyes slitting sly as a snake. "In exchange for a cutting from this fabulous tree?"

Sir Gareth looked from one sister to the other, trying to assess which was the least repellent. Una gave him a monocular wink, and Trina batted all three.

"Well, I, uh, I'm not too sure if I could speak for His Majesty on such a monumental matter. And of course, there is, uh, the question of the present queen. Of whom His Majesty is, uh, justly fond. But, uh, the King is really most insistent. I've been charged on my life to, uh . . ."

Dame Hedwig's brows knitted like two caterpillars, and the calculations continued once more. Her eyes sized up this strong young man with his fine square jaw and his deep blue eyes and his elegant blond moustache. After all, she thought, a knight was better than no one.

"And would *you*," she oozed, "be content to wed one of my darling daughters if she comes with a bough of fist-sized rubies in each hand? One for the King, and one for yourself in dowry?"

Sir Gareth juggled the alternatives, thinking how long a life could be—and yet how short in the event he failed. On the other hand, looks aren't everything, as all the stories said. Perhaps at least one of the horrid harpies had a heart, though their lecherous leers tended to make him doubt that. The choice was clear: a hapless union with a harridan—*with* an enduring dowry—*or* decapitation.

"Done!" Sir Gareth croaked.

"All right, girls," Dame Hedwig said. "Up the tree. Whichever of you brings down two branches becomes a knight's lady."

Well Una and Trina were up that tree like a pair of alley cats with their tails ablaze. Their garish skirts were slashed and sawed by the silver-scimitar leaves, and they pawed like women drowning to grasp a branch and wrench it from its sockets. But after half an hour they descended in defeat, their clothes in tatters and their faces and arms looking like victims of apprentice knife throwers.

"Oh, well," said Sir Gareth and turned away, realizing that fate had made the selection for him. All in all, he thought, perhaps death wasn't so difficult.

"*Wait!*" shouted Dame Hedwig. And Sir Gareth turned to see the mother holding a lovely servant girl by her golden hair. Dame Hedwig scowled a moment, then took in a grim breath, and shoved the girl toward the golden tree. Norma climbed lithely into the branches which seemed to embrace her, and the branch in her hand broke off willingly and dropped to the ground. And then another. Slowly she descended and stood before Sir Gareth, trying to hide her calloused hands.

Sir Gareth picked up the two branches with their silver leaves and ruby apples and smiled.

"No man is more fortunate than I," he said and took Norma's hand and led her to his steed. He lifted her onto its broad back, then heaved himself up behind, holding her in his strong arms. He jerked the reins, and the stallion turned and ambled out of the yard and onto the road away.

"Didn't even say goodbye, ungrateful trollop," Una grumbled.

"Now that she's had her comeuppance," Trina pursed, "I hope she remembers where she got her start."

"Don't worry, girls," Dame Hedwig sighed. "We always have our tree!"

And the three women turned to admire their securities. But even as they watched, the silver leaves began to pale to pewter, and then to grey, and finally they dusted down as ash. The ruby apples lost their hue and faded to rose, then to palish pink, then dried and drifted to the ground. Plump. Plump.

The three turned and watched the expectant faces of the unpaid servants and stableboys and cooks.

"Well, eat up!" Dame Hedwig hollered. "Come on, girls. We have to get started on next year's act."

It takes something greater than greed and agility
To uncover the key to true upward mobility.
The sole guarantee of a genuine gentility
Is a fine distillation of pride and humility.

11

FOOL'S GOLD

nce upon a time, long, long ago, when greed
was the cardinal virtue and thrift sure sign
of a sap, there lived this King Fluellen who
ruled Cornwall, the rear end of England. He
had all kingly qualities: arrogance, self-indulgence, and
the unflinching conviction you can be neither too rich
nor long satisfied. His queen, Mavis, was his equal: vain,
conniving, unforgiving, vengeful and a thorough virago.
They held one another in unreserved abhorrence and
tended to keep out of one another's affairs.

Fluellen's unfettered flings had siphoned the
treasury, and creditors' letters were less and less polite.

So he vowed, when the peasants were taxed to their last bear, he'd sell them abroad as slaves.

It was bruited that this barbarian was in obsessive pursuit of gold, so dubious looking men, motivated by the challenge of the chase and its rightful rewards, began showing up from all over. Their zest for the quest was whetted by the fact Fluellen was not only irresponsibly greedy but irresistibly gullible. Some said they could sniff buried treasure; others poked over hill and dale with dowsing rods; still others swore they could split trees and capture dryads in flasks and harness their power. Well, before long, that Cornwall looked like a brace of hurricanes had just taken their leave.

Next came men with long faces and unkempt hair railing, "Poppycock! No answer in druidic drivel, only in *science!* We must find this king the philosophers' stone which turns base metals into gold!" Tumbrils rumbled in daily, crammed with crucibles, condensers, and cannisters of chemicals. Before long, the laboratories were larger than the palace.

On they worked, digging, dowsing, grinding, boiling, rendering. And the treasury got emptier. And the king got edgier. And to the peasants, suicide looked easier and easier.

Then there strode into the palace a tall mysterious man with a white beard that tumbled to his toes. His black gown cascaded about him in silver runes and hieroglyphics, and on his conical hat blazed a silver sphinx. Anubis the Enigmatic.

That evening Anubis allowed Fluellen to attend on him. Edging through a maze of asps, cobras, copperheads, and one anaconda dozing with a serf-size lump halfway down its imposing length, Fluellen sat cautiously next to Anubis's divan, beside which his crocodile lay with one distrustful eye open.

"One dark midnight, long, long ago," Anubis began, "I crept into the pyramid of Great Osiris, and there I discovered the secret of the gem that changes all it touches to gold. The philosophers' stone!"

"Yes," Fluellen gasped. "Yes. Go on!"

"To distil the stone," he said, "we need a great many jewels."

"Don't give it another thought," Fluellen fluttered.

"Two hundred pounds of diamonds, twice that many rubies, four bushels of emeralds, and twenty barrels of pearls."

"Nothing. Nothing at all. My everyday crowns. Jewelry from my predecessors. If need be, my wife has . . ."

"No, no, no," Anubis tutted. "Unseemly." He rose majestically, signifying that the interview was concluded. "I shall meet you in the laboratory at . . . midnight!"

Fluellen made his way to the treasury in a delirium of joy.

At midnight, he hipped the last casque of pearls into the main laboratory, which held so much equipment from previous experiments that Anubis had all the paraphernalia he might desire.

Fluellen watched in awe as Anubis drew a druidic circle around jewels and equipment, marking zodiac signs in colored sands within its margin. The king coughed at the surfeit of incense, and as the hours dragged by he was close to fainting.

"It will be awhile, your majesty," Anubis said. "Take this draught and sleep awhile. I will wake you when Osiris appears."

So Fluellen curled up on a reeking stack of sacks and within an instant was poleaxed by nervous exhaustion.

He woke groggily, pawing around, unaware of where he was. Suddenly, he sat bolt upright. Full sunlight streamed through the smeary windows. Anubis was gone. So were the jewels.

He rose enraged, raring to roust his retainers for a country-wide search, when—in a shaft of sunlight—stood a young man in armor so shimmering the king thought he'd go blind.

"You have been ill-used, majesty," the deep voice rumbled. "Take this red jewel and rub it on your head and heart, and your wish will be fulfilled. You will find not only this betrayer, Anubis, but the secret of the philosophers' stone!"

Reeling with fatigue, confusion, and the need for revenge, King Fluellen rubbed the flashing crimson stone on his forehead and his breast. And he was instantly transformed!

Into a donkey.

Meanwhile, Queen Mavis was attending to obsessions of her own. Her scandalous liaisons were known to every bishop, burgher, and bogtrotter in the land. The only person in the realm unaware of her open-door policy was her gold-besotted husband, who would not have cared a whit that the paramour currently edging toward conquest of his spouse was the dazzlingly handsome Sir Hyperion of Llandudno, recently arrived.

Thus, while the king had been tending to his affairs that night, Queen Mavis had been tending to her own. Or to be specific, tending to Sir Hyperion of Llandudno. The servants had seen this gallant enter her chambers at a scandalously late hour, and he did not reemerge. The queen awoke and looked around for her *inamorato*. He was gone! So, in fact, were all her jewels.

But just as she was armoring her lungs to scream hell to heaven and wrench her curls from her royal head, a lovely maiden crowned with roses appeared in a shaft of sunlight.

"You have been ill-used, majesty," the light voice trilled. "Take this rose from my crown and put it in your bosom, and your wish will be fulfilled. You will find not only this betrayer, Hyperion, but the secret of true love."

Reeling with fatigue, confusion, and the need for revenge, Queen Mavis plunged the rose into her cleavage. And she was instantly transformed!

Into a goat.

That morning, the palace was in an uproar. Both highnesses had disappeared into thin air! They began a dutiful, if desultory, search of the palace and grounds, consoled in knowing that, if neither were found by suppertime, there'd be no slightest problem finding two better sovereigns, even in the village pub.

King Fluellen, his long ludicrous ears drooping, wandered the wilderness, heartsick. Then he saw a sur-passingly beautiful peasant girl trudging along burdened by a big sack. She stopped and scratched his ears, and he was instantly in love. She climbed on his back, and off he trotted until they came to a cave in the forest. The girl jumped down and called, "Gower! I'm here!" And a handsome young man emerged from the cave, embraced her and swung her round. "Ah, my Ruth," he said into her golden hair, in a surprisingly familiar voice. "You came so quickly."

"Thanks to this noble steed," she said, and stroking his back, she led King Fluellen into the cave and fed him some oats.

As Fluellen munched, he peered over his feedbag and saw on the table a white beard long enough to tumble to a man's toes. And a black cloak cluttered with silver signs. And the brocade costume of Sir Hyperion of Llandudno. And a suit of silver armor. And caskets and casques and canisters of his jewels.

"Isn't this more fun than playing 'Ralph Roister-Doister' in all those hamlets to a handful of hayseeds?" Gower said.

"And more profitable!" Ruth giggled as she emptied her sack of a diaphanous dress and a crown of roses. And all the Queen's jewels.

Trembling with rage, Fluellen rushed toward them, whinnying and flailing with his hooves. But the stalwart Gower plucked up a length of firewood and battered him balmy then dragged his unconscious carcass far out into the wilderness.

Fluellen came to his senses, lost, bewildered, and bitter of heart. For years he'd struggled to find ways to change lead into gold. But how to change a donkey back into a man? He pondered and pondered till finally he fell asleep. And while he slept, he dreamed he was king again! And a tall Egyptian was handing him a blazing stone. He took the stone and began touching it to everything in sight—tables, walls, manure piles, barns, roads—until everything in sight was blazing gold! Even peasants' hovels. And suddenly the king realized: Gold had no value anymore.

Fluellen awoke more heartsick than before, understanding at last that even worse than a half-dead donkey was a king who could turn anything into gold—even his head and heart. He headed toward a precipice, resolved to end it all. But as he reached the edge, he saw a single lily, white and lovely in the morning light. Within him rose the urge to eat this pure thing to purge his soul. So he ate the lily, and in a flash, he was transformed. He was a handsome, strapping peasant young man!

Reeling with joy, Fluellen made his way down the cliffs to a pleasant valley where he found a peasant cottage on a beautifully tended farm. He rapped shyly. The door opened, and he beheld a maiden of surpassing beauty, her blonde braids framing the face of an angel. Within, an old couple quietly gummed their bread.

"Forgive me," the king said. "My name is . . . Owen. I've lost my way. I was wondering if you might have some work for me."

"Yes, yes," the old man said, tottering to his feet, stroking his long white beard. "How fortunate we are, eh, mother? Just as we thought we could no longer survive, first Meg comes to our door, and now Owen! Come in, my boy, come in!"

So Fluellen began to cut the old couple's wood, clear new fields, tend their cattle. All day he labored, feeling the juice in his muscles, and each night slept the sleep of the just. And day by day his heart warmed at the sight of Meg, whose startling green eyes told him his interest was not unwelcome.

Finally, he could hold back no longer. "Meg," he said shyly, "I know I'm only a rude bumpkin, with little more to my name than the clothes on my back, but you've captured my heart. Could it possibly be that you . . . ?"

Meg flew into his arms. "Oh, yes, Owen, yes!" she whispered into his big shoulder. "But . . ."

"But what? Do you find me . . . unpleasant? Unpromising?"

"No, no! It's just that . . . well, I'm already married! I was once a queen. Truly. I know it sounds insane. My husband had no time for me, so I gave myself to rogues. One betrayed me; he stole all my jewels. But a beautiful maiden gave me a rose, and I touched it to my heart, and I was transformed into . . . a goat."

"But Meg!" Owen cried. "I was once a king! I was foolish, too! Obsessed with gold. A rogue betrayed me, too, and stole all my jewels. But a shining knight gave me a jewel, and I touched it to my heart, and I was transformed into . . . a donkey!"

"Fluellen?"

"Mavis?"

In the doorway behind them, stood the handsome Gower and the beautiful Ruth, smiling and holding chests of shimmering jewels.

"This is the final choice," Gower said. "You can have your jewels back. If that's what you want."

Meg and Owen stared at this mysterious pair.

"Will it be Fluellen and Mavis?" Ruth asked.

"Or Owen and Meg?" Gower asked.

They set the caskets of jewels on the doorsill and suddenly disappeared. The king and queen looked at the jewels, then at one another, and quietly stepped over them and walked into their cottage and closed the door.

And behind them the caskets of diamonds, rubies, emeralds, and pearls were suddenly transformed into seeds: corn, wheat, oats, rye. The philosophers' stone had finally been found.

In forging the fabled philosophers' stone,
The hesitant heart is the crucible
That flays and flenses the soul to the bone.
The essential is always inscrutable.

12

THE GOLDEN PESTLE

 nce upon a time, long, long ago, when honesty actually was the best policy, there lived this poor peasant named Angus in a house so poor that mice and fleas and cockroaches refused to take up residence there. His only treasure was his raven-haired daughter, Cristina, whose very presence made roses open their lips and sing. Even in January.

One day Angus said, "It's not right in a land so prosperous that we, who are willing and eager to work, should live from hand to mouth. I'm going to see young King Gustav and ask him for a piece of land." And off he went to the new young king, who had an open heart and hand, which showed his embarrassing lack of experience and his need to heed more cautious minds. King Gustav gladly gave Angus a fine plot of land, and the peasant and his lovely daughter were out in the field from sunrise to sunset, tilling and turning, plotting and planting, weeding and watering.

Then one day Cristina straightened her back and brushed the sweat from her rosy brow. The sun overhead glinted on something bright in the furrow at her feet. She got to her knees and pawed the dirt away. What was it but a mortar pot for mixing medicines and such. As big as a soup tureen and made of solid gold!

When she showed the mortar to her father, Angus was at first delighted. Then the smile faded from his face. "Since this is the King's land," he said, "we must give the mortar to him."

"But, Father, we haven't found the pestle, the rod the chemist uses to grind things in the mortar. That would be gold, too, wouldn't it? If you take the mortar to the King, he'll think we kept the golden pestle for ourselves."

"No, no, Cristina. See how generous King Gustav was to us. I couldn't sleep a wink in my bed if we kept this from him." So off Angus went to present the golden mortar to the King.

Meanwhile, young King Gustav had had some gruelling schooling from his more adult and avaricious advisors, so that when Angus presented himself and the golden mortar, the young man cocked his strong dark brow (as instructed) and said, "*A-a-and?*"

"And what, Your Majesty," Angus croaked.

"And the pestle," the King said.

"But we didn't find the pestle, Your Majesty."

An advisor with a face like a winter potato whispered in the young King's ear, and the King barked, "To the *dungeons!*"

Poor Angus lay there in the dungeon and droned, night and day, "Oh, if I'd only listened to my wise daughter! If only I'd listened to my wise daughter!" And since the King was still new at his job and therefore very few prisoners had been doomed to his dungeons, it began to nettle the nerves of the guards to hear this old man crying, over and over, "Oh, if only I'd listened to my wise daughter!" So they took their grievance to their commander until finally it reached the King himself. And the King summoned Angus to explain his pesky complaint.

"Oh, Your Majesty," Angus anguished, "my wise daughter told me not to bring the golden mortar till we'd found the golden pestle. Oh, if I'd only listened to my wise daughter!"

So King Gustav commanded that this wise daughter attend on him. And dressed in her best patched dress, Cristina presented herself to the King, who said, "Are you wise?"

Cristina blushed, and the King was much taken with her raven hair and bosky cheeks and comely form. "Your Majesty," she said, "I believe God gave women wits just as she gave them to men."

"She?" said the King imperiously (as instructed).

"A matter of perspective, I suppose."

The potato-faced advisor whispered in the King's ear, and the King said, "Then I want you to return here tomorrow, not clothed and not naked, not riding and not walking," and he turned to Potato Face to find if he'd gotten it right.

Next day, Cristina took off her clothes and wrapped herself in a fish net, so she was not clothed, nor was she naked. Then she tied the net to their donkey and bade him drag her along to the palace, so she was not walking, nor was she riding. When she arrived neither King nor Potato Face could deny she'd fulfilled their foolish request. And not only did the King release her father, but before his more adult and avaricious advisors could dissuade him, King Gustav impulsively asked Cristina to be his wise queen. And Cristina said she'd like that very much.

And so it was.

Some blissful years had passed, and King Gustav was reviewing his troops on parade, when there was a great brouhaha outside the palace gates. Two constantly feuding peasants had come delivering wood, Jasper with three wagons drawn by horses and Casper with three wagons drawn by oxen. And it seems as they arrived at the palace gates, one of Jasper's horses had—just like that—delivered herself of a foal. The poor foal dropped to the cobbles and, terrified of the light and noise, ran and hid among the three oxen. Jasper rumped his way through the ropey oxen and tried to retrieve his little horse. But Casper shoved him back, insisting one of his oxen had delivered the foal. Jasper sneered that, since an ox is male—and neutered at that, Casper's claim was laughable. But Casper did not laugh. Instead, he threw a haymaker right into Jasper's tough little gut. At which the friction flared like a forest fire with peasants pelting one another and passersby with milk cans, mortar, marble, masonry, maize, mulch, molasses, muck, mops, and manure from many sources, including mules.

Of course King Gustav stepped into the storm and becalmed it merely by raising his royal arms. When he had heard the claims, the King was forced to make a judgment. But since at the moment he was without benefit of his more adult and avaricious advisors, his solution was short of Solomonic. All he could stammer was, "Er, uh, 'Finders, keepers.' " And he walked away.

Now little Jasper had heard that Queen Cristina was not only grand and gifted but also gracious, because she had also come from peasant stock. So, hat in hand, he sought audience with the Queen and poured out his tale of his little foal.

The Queen looked at him kindly and said, "Now if I help you, you must promise not to betray me." And when Jasper said he'd rather die, she continued, "Tomorrow, take a great fishnet into the square outside the gates and, when the King rides out, stand there fishing, casting the net, hauling it in, emptying it out, and casting again." And then she told him what else to say.

Next morning when the King rode out, there was Jasper casting his net, hauling it in, emptying it out, casting again out over the dusty cobblestones. So the puzzled King sent a guard to ask what the wantwit was about. Jasper opened a toothless smile and said, "I'm fishing!" When the guard said a man can't fish where there's no water, Jasper grinned again: "As easy to get fish from cobbles as to get a foal from an ox." And all the peasants in their marketstalls began to howl with laughter.

Flushed with annoyance, not to mention a touch of deflation, King Gustav had Jasper hauled to him on his knees. "This disrespectful ruse was not your doing," he said, trying to look shrewd (as instructed). "Whose idea was this ridiculous prank?"

But Jasper folded his spindly arms across his washboard chest and stuck out his stubbly chin.

So King Gustav nodded, and his soldiers began to belabor Jasper's head and shoulders and back and bottom, beating him like a balky mule again and again, until finally poor Jasper managed to mumble: "God forgive me, the Queen."

Well, public embarrassment for a person of power is one thing. Public betrayal is quite another. So King Gustav stormed back to the palace and slammed into the Queen's salon.

"What *right* have you to connive against me!" he stormed, his black brows bristling. "It's . . . it's *treason!* Go back to your peasant's hovel! I un-queen you!"

A tear trickled down Cristina's lovely cheek. She curtseyed and said, "As my husband commands. But . . ."

"But what?" the King glowered, wishing he had waited or at least had a chance to ask some advice.

"If I could only look about the palace and choose just one thing to take with me, something precious that would remind me of what once I was."

"Well, uh, yes, uh, of course," King Gustav grumbled and strode away, unable to watch her weep.

Queen Cristina wiped away her tear and smiled. Then she summoned her maid and said, "I want you to help me prepare a flagon of ale for His Majesty's luncheon." And the two set about their business giggling like little girls.

When the overheated King sat down to luncheon, he reached for his flagon and took a deep draft to drown the strong suspicion he'd acted the fool. Within moments, he fell forward, snoring facedown in his filet of sole.

Queen Cristina crept from behind the curtains and summoned the servants standing by. She handed them a fine brocade coverlet and told them to wrap the King carefully and bring him out to her carriage. Dismissing the servants, she climbed atop the box, took the reins in her own hands, and she drove her snoring spouse to her father's house.

The astonished Angus carried the King into the house and laid him in Cristina's old little bed. And at that moment, the King came drowsily awake and looked around.

"Good God, where am I?" he asked.

Cristina smiled down on him and said, "My King, you told me I could bring away with me one thing I found precious in the castle. And there was nothing more precious to me there than you. So I brought you with me."

Tears started in the King's eyes, and he said, "What a fool I've been, haven't I? And you did bring me something far more precious than that golden pestle long ago. A wise wife."

And the Queen, wisely, smiled in silence.

So King Gustav brought her back to his palace and not only reinstated his Queen but made her his chief counsellor. And ordered, without advice from anyone, that henceforth Potato Face be employed to muck out the royal stables.

And so it was.

When posed a prickly problem of priority.
It's prudent to defer to someone wiser.
But office doesn't make one an authority.
Sometimes one's misprized bride's his best advisor.

13

PRINCE HARRY THE HOG

nce upon a time, long, long ago, when the unexpected was the usual thing, there was this King named Egbert, whose queen was expecting their first child. One afternoon while Queen Priscilla dozed in her garden, three enchantresses happened by on their way to a high-level meeting: Pristina, handmaid to the Goddess of Beauty, Serena, handmaid to the Goddess of Peace, and Gangrena, handmaid to the Goddess of Irritation. Gangrena's patents included hangnails, paper cuts, poison ivy, mosquitoes, and underclothing that creeps up on the wearer. She was also geared to take over distribution of blaster boxes, chewing gum, motorbikes, graffiti markers, commercial interruptions, and third-class mail, once they were invented.

Noticing the queen's quite obvious delicate condition, Serena suggested they pause and bestow gifts on this unborn boy and his mother. Pristina smiled, "May this mother never encounter one who will harm her, and her son be the handsomest man in the world." Serena said, "May this mother never encounter one who will insult her, and her son be trustworthy, loyal, helpful, friendly, courteous, kind, obedient, cheerful, *et cetera*."

Gangrena wrestled her overtaxed girdle into place and glared at her two milksop sisters, who had left her very little to offer in the way of birth wishes. "All right," she snarled, "may this mother be the most long-suffering of women—*and* may she have plenty of occasions to exercise it, and may this boy who is going to be the handsomest man in the world be born in the skin of a pig."

Then she dusted her hands and snapped, "Let's go. Or we'll miss the opening speeches you both hate so much." And her sisters shook their lovely heads and followed in her waspish wake.

The queen awoke, puzzling over a dream. Shimmering presences, and one slipping a sweet baby into the skin of a pig.

No more aware than that of their progeny's prospects, the king and queen awaited the day. Imagine their surprise when she gave birth to a bouncing, sweetly smiling, ruddy-faced child—who looked exactly like a pig.

King Egbert was of a mind to put this misborn child to death to save his sweet queen the shame. Not to mention himself. Or the godawful question of succession. On the other hand, the child *was* theirs and really rather cute, once one got used to the big eyes, the pointy ears, the dixie-cup nose, the jowls. So they bowed to their fate, and they named the new prince Hereford.

Queen Priscilla nursed Prince Harry as tenderly as a normal child. She bathed him, caressed him, smooched his unsightly snout, and spoke goo-goo talk about as intelligible to your ordinary hog as to your ordinary infant. And as he grew, he displayed intelligence, trustworthiness, loyalty, helpfulness, *et cetera*. The one area in which the prince might be faulted, however, was everyday etiquette and cleanliness. From the days when he was able to totter about on his tiny back trotters, Harry got into everything. He heedlessly knocked over antique tables and their burden of vases and statues, all of considerable antiquity, and he was known to snout around the servants quite expectedly. Worst of all, he rolled delightedly in the muck and came home with his silken playsuits caked with gobbets of mud and smelling of swill. Understandable, of course, in a small child, but as he grew into adolescence, unnerving. Not to mention the expense.

Then one day, Prince Harry, who had become quite thick-chested and husky, shouldered into his mother's chambers with a request that nearly precipitated Queen Priscilla into cardiac arrest. "Mother," he said, "I want to get married."

When the queen's ladies-in-waiting had with some difficulty revived her and she sat staring blearily at the prince, he made his request again, "Mother, I want to get married."

"My dear Harry," said the queen muzzily, "you can't be entirely serious. Who would marry someone who looks like a pig? Dear, you're the sweetest young man I've known, and I love you dearly, but you must confess you're rather . . . ungainly, and a touch . . . sloppy, and—not to put too fine a point on it—unless the servants keep after you, you do tend to . . . well, smell."

"But Mother," he persisted, "I've seen the poor Widow Wither who has three ravishing daughters, Beulah, Bianca, and Bella. Her husband died in terrible debt to the royal banks. Unless someone helps them, they'll all have to go to debtors' prison. I'm sure you could speak to her. I know I'm no prize, but perhaps I'm more promising than prison."

"Oh, Harry, my dear, I really don't . . ."

"I understand," the prince said and ambled sadly away.

For days the queen watched poor Harry moping about the palace, taking no delight in even the muckiest days, losing weight, and often she'd see a tear roll down his hairy cheek. Finally, she could endure it no longer and summoned the widow, on the slightest chance she might mend her son's sorrowing heart.

The Widow Wither sat in her patched Sunday best, straight as poker on the lip of her chair, eyeing and envying the intimidating luxury to right and left. But when the queen made her proposal, the woman's beady eyes flared like floodlights.

"I quite realize that Prince Harry *resembles* a hog," the queen said, "but your daughter would eventually be *queen,* you know. Queen, or, if I may be somewhat indelicate, convict?"

The Widow Wither huffed and hemmed and hawed but eventually realized she was in a standoff and averred she would try. When she returned home and told her eldest, Beulah, of this somewhat circumscribed opening to the good life for them all, Beulah went into a titanic tantrum, hurling anything unpawned that came to hand, shrieking and tearing her hair. But when her mother described debtors' prison, the filth, the foul smells, vermin and rats, Beulah settled for snorts and sniffles. And when her mother showed her the dress the queen had given her in which to meet her porcine intended, she became nearly tractable.

The following day, Beulah and her mother presented themselves at the palace, Beulah radiant in her new finery. The queen sent for the prince, who had been disconsolately snouting tulip bulbs out of the formal gardens, and he entered her chamber with blobs of soil sliding from his hairy sides.

"Harry, my dear," she said. "We have found you a wife."

Well, Prince Harry's heart exploded with joy! He ran to his fair-faced fiancee and capered about her, licking and nuzzling her cheeks, and griming and gobbeting her gorgeous gown.

"My *dress!*" Beulah squealed.

Prince Harry backed off, abashed. "I'm so sorry. I . . . I was just so happy. And we have so many more. You'll have a different dress for every hour you live, if you like. I'm so sorry."

Beulah and her mother returned home, the girl wondering if debtors' prison might not be a more appealing alternative. Or she could run off and join the gypsies. But the Widow Wither had a plan, in service of which she presented Beulah with a lethally long stiletto. On the nuptial night, when the portly prince entered her bed, she was to slash his throat and claim he had tried to devour her. No one dare claim Beulah hadn't lived up to her part of the bargain.

In the interests of propriety, the wedding festivities were limited to the couple, parents, and priest. And after a brief supper during which the beatific bridegroom made rather a mess of himself, the couple retired to their nuptial chamber. The bride withdrew within her curtained bed, and when the eager prince clambered through the draperies, he froze in horror.

"Beulah, dearest," he gulped, "why do you have that knife?"

"To cut your throat with, you filthy sack of suet!" Beulah screamed and lunged at the horrified Harry.

In terror, he tried to fend her off, slashing out with his trotters, butting her away, squealing and kicking and sideswiping his rump about in frenzy. Moments later, he stopped, huffing and wheezing. And he looked down at the bed. There lay Beulah, battered and bloody and undeniably dead.

Summoned by the unseemly sounds of a marital melee, the king and queen burst in the door and saw the gory outcome of the couple's first-ever venture into happily ever after.

"She tried to *kill* me!" Harry snorted. "On our *wedding* night. See? The knife is still in her hand."

Fortunately, due to the truncated manner of the nuptials, the incident was easily hushed up. Any servants privy to the problem were given handsome bonuses and prominent positions in the king's possessions in Patagonia. But there did remain the duty of informing the Widow Wither of her daughter's deplorable demise. Along with the unfortunate matter of her thwarted attempt to dispatch the future king to Kingdom Come.

The Widow Wither, being a former woman of the world, saw that once again she had checkmated herself, so she agreed that the pig prince might marry her second daughter, Bianca, provided no charges were forthcoming. As one might expect, the scenario repeated itself nearly page-for-page: the operatic refusal, the dire descriptions of the dungeons, the reluctant consent, the succinct ceremony. But this time the widow saw a knife might be a touch unprofessional, not to say a dead giveaway, so she slipped Bianca a deadly dosage of paralyzing poison. But when the poor girl saw her spouse's spatulate snout slobbering through the curtains of her bed, she hastily decided to cut her losses and downed the poisoned posset herself.

Prince Harry, naturally, was a touch depressed at this turn of events and the diminishing margin of his marriageability. So the queen summoned Widow Wither again, along with Bella, her final daughter and final chance. But when the queen made her offer, Bella blushed and said, "I'd be honored, my lady."

Accustomed to more theatrical response, the queen and widow looked incredulously at her, pink and delicate as a rose.

"There is no other choice," Bella said, "for my mother and myself but the prince or prison. That would be reason enough. But no one has ever known Prince Harry to be anything but gentle, generous, and good-hearted. Many a woman with a handsomer husband who preens like a peacock would be happy to exchange him for a kindly pig. I am quite content."

Chastened by his previous frightening forays into wedded bliss, Prince Harry entered his mother's salon less unsightly and quite a bit more hesitant. He approached lovely Bella and offered his best attempt at a courtly bow. And fell on his face.

"Prince," Bella said. "Would you like to lay your head on my lap awhile? You seem so sad."

Prince Harry laid his lolling dewlaps on Bella's knee. She stroked his brow tenderly, and a tear ran down his bristly cheek.

After the wedding, Prince Harry slipped carefully into Bella's chamber, his piggy eyes darting to left and right, hoping not to make too great a fool of himself this time, but also somewhat wary of lethal weapons. But Bella lay demurely on her bed, patting the covers and bidding her unseemly spouse to lie beside her. Shyly he laid his horrid head on the pillow and turned away from her lest she be frightened. But she pulled the bedclothes up around him and held him quietly in her arms.

Next morning, Queen Priscilla crept silently into the room, dreading yet another departed daughter-in-law. But there she saw Princess Bella sitting up against the pillows, her face brighter than the morning sun on the window sill.

"But . . . ," the queen stammered.

"Gentle queen," Bella smiled, "I have married the handsomest, tenderest, sweetest man alive."

"But . . ."

For days the queen puzzled over this unlikely turn of events, happy her son was jubilant all day long and the new princess radiantly joyful, but still wondering if she hadn't married her prince off to a very strange girl indeed. She paced her chambers, pondering, probing, pummeling her memory for a clue just outside her grasp.

Then in a flash she remembered her dream: three filmy lights hovering over her, slipping a beautiful child into the skin of a pig. Honest love had worked a change in her son, wiped out whatever wicked whim had encased his good soul in such a frightful form. And the queen knew just what to do.

That night, when all the palace slept, she crept into the young couple's room. Pawing through the dark, she found her way to the curtained bed, and—just as she'd suspected—at the side of the bed lay the filthy, bristling skin of a pig. And in the bed, folded in one another's arms, lay Bella and a young man whose beauty took his mother's breath away.

Quickly, Queen Priscilla snatched up the horrid skin and ran breathlessly to her rooms and cut it to shreds, burning the pieces in a brazier. Then she sat in her great chair, smiling and rocking quietly, waiting for the dawn.

Cliches are such stayers because they are true,
Like "Beauty is only skin deep."
The opposite often is verified, too:
That beauty disguises a creep.

14

THE BATTLE OF THE BASSINETS

 nce upon a time, long, long ago, when Consistency and Spontaneity had not yet resolved their differences, there lived this exemplary king named Justin and his delightful queen, Capriole. The royal spouses loved one another to distraction, though often at cross-purposes.

King Justin's deepest desire was to maintain unquestionable fairness in his realm. In fact, King Justin had conceived the eccentric goal of making all of his subjects happy. His advisors snickered in whispers about the idiocy of such a proposition. Anyone with a room-temperature IQ knew the goals of kingship were to achieve unquestioning obedience in one's subjects, unlimited wealth in one's treasury, territory one could not catalogue or cross in a lifetime, and the proper balance between riotous living and a long-lived liver. But the noble king struggled on against the tide of conventional wisdom.

Queen Capriole was equally single-minded in regard to fairness, but its scope was limited to the unquestionable fairness of her own person. Not only was she bountifully blessed with beauty of face and figure, but she was fanciful, tenderhearted, whimsical, and given to the most delightful impulses, which made her the darling of her king, court, and kingdom. When she set a candle to the beard of the Wazier of Ophir, for instance, the court laughed for days, though trade with Ophir dwindled drastically.

The flip-side to her winsome unpredictability, however, was her penchant for Achillean sulks, which usually lasted six months of every year, not consecutively. Both her miasmal moods and madcap merriment often outran the reins of common sense, often verging on the dangerous and—in the minds of the more puritan—the downright looney. Queen Capriole was, indeed, what a later more analytical and less compassionate age might call a certifiable manic-depressive.

The great shadow that often clouded Queen Capriole's sunny disposition was that, although she had willingly rendered the marriage debt more often than your average rabbit, she had yet to render an heir to her doting king. Since it was unthinkable that she herself be the cause of her aridity, in her darkest grumps she railed operatically at the ineptitude of anyone even remotely connected to her lack of fecundity, from her long-suffering apothecary to her progenitrixes all the way back to Eve. She even hinted (but only to the unbreachable bosom of her confessor) at some inadequacy in the sexual circuitry of King Justin himself.

Queen Capriole besieged every woman in the kingdom from the Archmidwife-Sorceress to the lowliest peasant wife—who would dearly have loved to be just as ignorant of the secret she so sedulously sought. The only response she received from those she bedeviled was a beetling of brows, since anyone in the kingdom above the age of five seemed perfectly conversant with what it took to make what she wanted to happen . . . happen.

Of course, the queen also consulted physicians at every coloration of the spectrum. She dosed herself with potions, pastilles, panaceas, and placebos: calomel, cascara, leptandra, peyote, and mashed parts of various vermin too sickmaking to retail further.

Nor did she eschew the possibility of transcendent influences on her barren state, and thus she consulted priests, rabbis, druids, shamans, warlocks, mullahs, ramwats, popes and antipopes, each of whom exhorted prayer, fasting, vows, and pilgrimages—not to mention substantial donations. She submitted to spells, sweats, and conjurations and stumbled from room to room bedizened with amulets, talismans, fetishes, rabbit's feet, and what a squint-eyed peddler had insisted was Alladin's Lamp itself, for which the king blithely paid a sultan's ransom. No whim of his wife was too wasteful or wild.

At last, the queen felt a quite incontrovertible twinge in her royal tummy, and—although she was unable to ascertain which of the myriad simples had proven effective—she rushed from courtier to chambermaid to scullion in rapture and entwined each in pythonic embrace. Indeed, anyone she encountered on her rapturous rampage risked asphyxiation.

Of course, everyone in the kingdom wanted a boy, since a male child evaded epic rats' nests regarding succession. But with predictable unpredictability, Queen Capriole insisted that the first-fruits of her so-long-fallowness would be a girl. Although throughout their marriage the king had deferred to his spouse's every slightest vagary, this was a choice that would affect history, and thus he argued manfully to the contrary. But Queen Capriole responded coldly that, since the king's part in this enterprise had been remarkably brief and the rest of the process remained solely in her hands (so to speak), he could go about his business and she would go about hers.

But the king persisted. The queen's face squinched tighter and tighter: her brows circumflexed into crabbed caterpillars above her agate eyes; her mouth pinched into a miser's purse; her lovely chin alchemized to cold steel—until the queen-mother-to-be finally imploded into the great grandmother of all sulks, into which she folded herself for weeks.

Distraught at his beloved's rejection, the king consulted the Archmidwife who calmed his royal apprehensions and told him all this was quite natural. If a woman is persnickety now and then, she argued, it was only a sort of safety valve to deflate her husband's olympian ego. Capriole had withdrawn like a flower from his wintry blasts, and as soon as he stopped opposing her fancies, she would open her sprightly soul to him once again like a butterfly emerging from her cocoon. "Be sweet to her," she purred. "Apologize. Approach her, sovereign to sovereign, seeking peace. Cajole. Woo. In short, grovel."

Under the king's wooing and cooing, Capriole's resistance slowly began to melt, and gradually her exuberance reappeared so that it was obvious to all that the wife, as she by duty must, had finally yielded to her husband's wishes. Or so they thought.

During a great state dinner at which anyone who was anyone in the known world was in attendance, the queen rose to her tiny feet and spoke with unsurpassable sweetness. "My liege lord and lifemate," she said, "has *ordered* me to produce a male child, and of course I would never *dream* of doing otherwise. You may all rest assured this royal child I carry within my sacred precincts will be a prince." She sat down amidst tumultuous applause, not only for her welcome news but for her admirable wifely submission. Several days later, the Archmidwife confirmed the fact and announced solemnly to the visibly relieved Royal Council that the queen would, indeed, deliver them their prince.

Privately, however, she crept into the queen's quarters and whispered into her ear: "You will have a princess," for which the Archmidwife was extravagantly rewarded.

Her Highness became the soul of uxoriousness, speaking only of her joy at her incipient son and his deeds of derring-do and diplomacy and the dynasty he would assure. She and her ladies set themselves like spinning spiders to prepare a blue wardrobe for the princeling, and the color pink was banished from the palace precincts. She enjoined all the bewildered court philosophers to prepare learned lectures to commence before the prince was even weaned. When the king questioned the effectiveness of such early intellectual challenge, the queen responded with unaccustomed acuity, "Wouldn't it be better to have your son hear all the dumb things they have to say before the child is able to understand them? If he hears them after he has the slightest sense at all, they'll send him round the bend." And the queen smiled, hardly able to contain her eagerness to see the faces of the royal counsellors when they first lifted the royal nappy and saw the truth for themselves.

At last, with unsurpassable ecstasy, the queen felt her first hint that the time had come. The palace was in chaos, with maids and footmen and equerries careening into one another on a thousand useless errands, while the king paced outside the room of accouchement like a minotaur in a maze. At last, the Archmidwife poked her whiskery face out the door and whispered to the king, "It's a boy!" The king's feet could scarcely glue themselves to the gilded floor. But a moment later, she was back, "It's a girl!" The king was ecstatic: both his wife's wishes and his own had been fulfilled! But the most remarkable thing about these two miraculous twins was that they were absolutely identical, dressed in the powder-blue their mother and her ladies-in-waiting had fabricated for the expected prince.

The queen was unexpectedly chastened by this unusual experience of having both lost and won at the same time. To make amends to her husband for being so obdurate, she focused her entire attention on the infant prince against whom she had been so firmly set, completely neglecting her daughter. And the king, guilty over his insistence on a son against his wife's wishes, doted on the young princess to the exclusion of her brother.

The day of the children's baptism arrived, and the whole court had gathered in glorious array, with the servants standing in gilded attention, and the courtyard crowded with peasants in their Sunday best. Before the sacrament began, the Archmidwife-Sorceress arose and said, "Before these sacred waters take these children from the realm of sorcery into the realm of spirit, what qualities would you have me bestow on this prince and princess? And what name shall each child have?"

That's when all hell broke loose. There was an electric and escalating altercation between King Justin and Queen Capriole about which child should be wise and which winsome, which direct and which devious, which ingenuous and which ingenious. When that donnybrook waned, the two royal contenders segued effortlessly into a dispute over the children's names. The object of their discord was, of course, not to determine what was right for the children but who could make the other submit.

"*STOP!*" the Archmidwife averred at last. "Your royal majesties each take *one* of the infants and make your wishes for that child."

So, resolutely, the king snatched up the infant prince and clutched him to his oaken chest; single-minded as a madwoman, the queen grasped the princess to her upholstered bosom.

"I want this child," Queen Capriole said with a vinegar smile, "to have all *your* qualities, my king: prudence, predictability, productivity, practicality, profundity, and propriety. And her name shall be Prudens!"

With a feral grin, King Justin said, "I want this child to have all *your* qualities, my queen: capricious, captivating, captious, capering, and capsizing everything in sight! And his name shall be Caprice!"

At that moment, a cynical seer could foretell the future of the kingdom: Prince Caprice would be so like his mother that he would drive the woman mad; he would destroy the royal bureaucracy in order to make it simple enough for him to comprehend; he would turn the kingdom to chaos trying to reform it. On the other hand, Princess Prudens would be so intelligent and wise that even the most impoverished prince would shudder to contemplate marriage with her; her wisdom in contrast to her simpleton sibling would incite all sorts of cabals, conspiracies, and collusions to overthrow the impulsive prince and install the prudent princess. In short, the whole kingdom was going to be shot to hell.

So much for doomsayers. The two royal infants, you recall, were born with identical faces, fingers, and physiques—at least when covered by their identical baptismal dresses. The queen in her hot-headed haste had, in truth, picked up her son, and the king in his unrighteous rage had picked up his daughter.

And Prince Prudens grew up to be a king of uncommon acuity, compassion, and control. Princess Caprice became a beauty even more ravishing than her mother (if that was either conceivable or tenable), with the same lightsome airs and impetuous whims, and she forced every one of her many suitors to lose either their lives or their fortunes or their wits.

The gist of this frivolous folktale we owe
To the eminent philosophe Jean-Jacques
    Rousseau.
Its burden is simple but sometimes confuses:
If either spouse triumphs, then everyone loses.

15

TRISTRAM, THE MASTER THIEF

nce upon a time, long, long ago, when robbing the poor to give to the rich was more commonplace than today, there lived these poor old peasants, Aldwyn and Winnie, in a hut no larger than a closet. One day, when they were resting their withering bones in the afternoon sun before another assault on the bindweed and burdock and burrs against whom they waged daily feud for their food from their garden, a richly dressed young man rode up and smiled down at them. He was firm-jawed, and his sleek moustache framed a mouth that brooked no doubt.

"Ah, friends," the young man said, "I've traveled long and hard, and perhaps I'm lost. I was wondering, since I haven't eaten this day, if you might have a potato pancake to spare for a fool who's lost his way."

"My Lord . . . ," Aldwyn began, bowing.

"No, no, sir," the young man said. "Just a poor wayfarer. My name is Tristram."

Aldwyn and Winnie exchanged a slow, sad look.

"I'm sorry," Tristram said, jumping from his horse. "Did I say something wrong? I'm truly sorry."

"No, no, sir," Winnie said. "We . . . our son had that name."

"Tristram? Now that's a coincidence, isn't it?"

"Ah, yes, sir," Aldwyn sighed, "but our Tristram's gone this many a year. We heard he's gone bad. A lovely, handsome boy, he was, with charm to whisk the whiskers off a witch. But filled with this mischievous mirth, you know? Clever he was, and knowing. At last he ran away, and we've heard but rumors since."

"I'm sorry to hear that," Tristram said. "But . . . ?"

"Ah, yes," Winnie sighed and heaved to her heavy feet. "A potato pancake! The old fella and me was just wondering whether there was still some work left locked in our bones, or whether we might just have a wee wet o' tea. And you just made up our minds, young sir! Sit there awhile. I'll be but a minute."

While Winnie went into the hut to cook their supper, Aldwyn and Tristram stayed in the shade a bit, but Aldwyn had worked all his life and was not a man to sit too long. As Tristram spoke, he fiddled with the plants at his feet, tying one to a stick he had jammed in beside it, to make it grow straight and tall.

"That plant over there," Tristram said. "It seems to have grown quite crooked. Why did you never tie it to a stake like the one you're doing now?"

"Ah, sir, you know something of plants, do you? But, truth to tell, I've neglected that one far too long. I'll have to pull it up, I suspect. It's grown too knotted to save."

"Like your son, Tristram, I suspect," the young man said.

Just then Winnie came to the door and heard what the two had said. The three looked quizzically at one another, and then Winnie's mouth fell open. "Child?" she cried.

Tristram's handsome face nodded shyly, and Winnie ran and enfolded him in her arms. Aldwyn was a deal more hesitant, his hands and his heart more than willing to embrace the boy, but his head putting limits to his love.

"Father," Tristram said, his arm encircling his mother's comfortable waist, "what you've heard is partly true. I've become a thief. In fact, a master thief. No, no, no, before you hurl me out as you did last time! I rob the rich and give to the poor. Except perhaps a slight bit more, as some small fee for services rendered."

"So," said Aldwyn, "it's a Robin Hood I've spawned."

"Not that idealistic," Tristram grinned. "But along those general lines. No one in the world *needs* a million ducats. And paupers' children do. But, I confess, I'm no pauper myself."

"A thief is a thief," Aldwyn gruffed. "If our lord, Count Cedric, hears of this, he'll not take you in his arms, as he did when he stood godfather for you! He'll give you the gift of a yard of rope to dance in the air with."

"Father," Tristram said, "if Mother will give me tea, I'll present myself to Count Cedric this very evening. And I guarantee, before the week is out, he'll have given me pardon."

So the three went into the hut and had their tea, Winnie like a mother newly-delivered, fussing and fondling her boy, and Aldwyn grumping and grousing, but half-happy his boy was home.

That evening, Tristram presented himself at the castle and asked to speak to Count Cedric. He was a sleek man, with rawboned cheeks and jet black hair but a glint of the human left in his humorless ice-blue eyes. He greeted the young stranger warmly, sure from his clothes he must be of some importance. But when Tristram revealed who he was, Count Cedric went pale for a time, steepling his fingers under his goatee and pondering.

"You put me in an unenviable position, young Master Tristram," the Count said. "On the one hand, you are my godson whom I'm sworn before God to protect. On the other, you are a felon—and let's not mince words about motives. As the law in this shire, I should have you horsewhipped and hanged. Why didn't you just pass us by?"

"I wanted to ease my parents' final years. That is my trade, you see," Tristram grinned. "And I don't like being underhanded with friends. Can we strike a bargain, Your Grace?"

"Bargain?"

"Let me ransom my hide with my head. Think of three tasks, as difficult as you can, and if I can't perform them, do with me as you will. If I succeed, you will see that my parents never want for food or decent lodging."

The Count reflected a moment. "Very well, then. First, you must steal my horse, which I warn you is always guarded. Then you must steal the bedclothes from my bed without my knowing, as I sleep. Ah, and my wife's ruby ring as well. And third . . . ?" He paused a moment more. "Yes, third, you will kidnap that pompous Parson Phineas and his silly sexton, Sam, and give them the fright of their lives. I've been trying to deflate those gasbags for years. Mark you. Fail in even one task, and you can forget any scruples I have about your untimely demise."

So next evening Tristram went into the town and bought the clothes of an old peasant woman and put them on, and he bound an old babushka round his hair. He stained his face with iodine water, hollowed his eyes and cheeks with charcoal, and blackened his teeth. Then he filled a cask with Spanish wine, spiked with a healthy dose of sleeping potion. He put the cask in a basket bound to his back and began to totter toward the castle, hacking and spitting and snorting the drips from his nose. When he crossed the town square, he saw a convict's corpse swinging from the gallows with a placard round his neck: "Murderer." The old lady crossed herself and sighed aloud, "Ah, man's wicked ways!"

When she came to the Count's stable, some soldiers were lying around a fire, playing cards to kill the time. "Hey, old mother," a soldier called, "come warm your brittle bones." So the old woman hobbled over to them and settled with a sigh. "And what's in the cask, old dame?" a soldier asked.

"Red wine with a better bite than I have," the old lady cackled. "For a few coppers, I'd let you have a cup."

So the soldiers fell to, and Tristram filled their cups and pocketed their pennies. Then the soldiers pointed into the stables to the grooms. "Hey, old girl, perchance you can pick a pocket or two in there," one said, a bit muzzily, then dropped over and dozed on his comrade's shoulder. So the old woman carried her cask into the stable. One of the grooms sat atop the Count's horse, and another held its bridle. So she poured them each a cup of wine and watched them drink.

Slowly they sagged. Tristram eased the reins from the groom's hands and put a rope in its place. But how to get the rider off without a hoot and holler? So he rigged a rope round the groom's waist and threw it over a roofbeam, hauling him into the air, and there he hung, smiling in his sleep and swimming in air. Tristram bound the horse's iron-shod feet in rags and slowly led the horse past the sleeping guards, and away he flew.

Next morning Tristram showed up bright and early, just as the Count was going out for his ride. "Ah!" he grinned. "I warmed up your horse for you, Your Grace. As you can see, your grooms and soldiers are otherwise occupied."

Count Cedric fought against a grin. "Well and good," he growled. "But you've two more tasks to do, and you won't find them as easy as this."

When Countess Candace went to bed that night, she closed her hand tightly on her ruby ring. But Count Cedric smiled and patted his pistol, "The doors are all bolted, my dear. I will sit here all the night, and if the blighter tries the window, I will blast him to hell. That should soothe my scruples."

Meanwhile, Tristram had gone to the gallows and retrieved the murderer's corpse. He crept up below the tower window and raised a ladder and, holding the corpse before him, up he climbed. Slowly he eased the murderer's head up into the casement, and the Count, dozing in his chair by his snoring wife, saw the head silhouetted against the moonlight. He raised his pistol and fired. And Tristram heaved the corpse away.

Countess Candace awakened in terror and began to scream. And as the Count was calming her, Tristram scooted down the ladder and hid in the brush.

"Now, now, my dear," the Count said, rubbing his hysterical wife's hands. "He deserved what he got. Caught in the act. But . . ." The Count hesitated. "He was my godson. More a rascal than a villain. And I would not want his parents disgraced. I have it! I'll bury him in the garden, and no one will be the wiser." So he climbed out onto the ladder and scurried down, picked up the corpse, and hauled it off to the flowerbeds.

As a cloud mantled the moon and cast darkness over the garden, Tristram scooted back up the ladder and whispered through the window, "Wife," he said. "I don't want to bury the lad so brutally. Give me the sheet to wrap him in." So Countess Candace groped to the window and handed the bedclothes to him. Tristram chuckled. "I feel a fit of mischief myself, my dear. Since the lad was so cocksure he could steal your ruby ring, give it to me, and I'll bury him with it. Poetic justice, no? I'll buy you another, twice as large."

"Cedric, are you sure? Oh, well," she said and handed him the ring. "But do take care. Running around out there in your bare feet, you sound as if you're coming down with a cold."

So down Tristram leaped, and off he ran and was home in his bed before the Count had finished burying him.

Imagine the Count's face next morning when Tristram's corpse came sauntering in, the bedclothes neatly folded in one hand and the ring in the palm of the other. And out he walked, leaving Count Cedric behind him unable to rejoin his teeth.

That night Tristram rode his horse to the village church, two burying shrouds across his lap. He dismounted in the graveyard and hauled two sacks from his crupper, one filled with live crabs and the other with candle stubs. One by one, he took the crabs from the sack, lit a candle and stuck it on each crab's back with the melted wax, until the churchyard was filled with slowly moving lights. Then just as the church clock tolled midnight, he pulled a long black hooded cloak from his saddle and climbed atop a gravestone and began to preach.

"Ah, you sinners!" he cried. "The end of time has come! I am St. Peter, and I'm here to separate the just from the unjust! Whoever will come with me to heaven, must not come unshrouded. Come! Come!"

Inside the vestry, Parson Phineas and Sexton Sam stumbled from their beds. "Did you hear what I heard?" the Parson asked through the long length of his aristocratic nose.

"I thought I was dreaming," Sexton Sam squeaked.

"Well, we must be on our way," the Parson sneered. "If *any*one in this wicked town is worthy of heaven, you and I are. Or at least . . ."

So the two scuttled out into the moonless night and crept into the cemetery, alive with moving lights.

"Oh, my little brothers," the darkly shrouded eminence on the monument moaned, "make haste! The time is nigh! Quick! You must not enter heaven clad in worldliness. Strip off your earthclothes and enter your shrouds! I, St. Peter, *command* it!"

So Parson Phineas and Sexton Sam stripped to their skinny shanks and shimmied into the rough shrouds. Quick as a blink, Tristram bound the mouths of the shrouds and tied them to the pommel of his saddle and bumped them off toward the castle.

"The way to heaven is rocky indeed," the Parson mumbled.

As Tristram crossed a stream, Sexton Sam murmured, "My feet are wet! We're crossing the River Styx! Are we going to hell?"

Finally Tristram arrived at the castle and began to drag the two sacks up the steps, bumping their domes on each.

"No!" exclaimed Parson Phineas with glee. "We've reached the steps of heaven! We're going up, you see? Soon we'll be within the Celestial Court! How glad they'll be to welcome me!"

Up the circular staircase Tristram grunted, hauling the sacks up and up until he was on the roof. One by one he lifted them into the pigeon coop and bolted the door behind them.

"Ah, Sam!" Parson Phineas crooned. "It's true! Just listen to the angels' wings!"

Next morning, bright and early, Tristram presented himself once more at the castle.

Count Cedric cocked a quizzical eye when he saw the young man empty-handed. "I half-hoped you'd pull this one off. I did so look forward to seeing those two pompous asses brought down to earth. Oh, dear. You haven't killed them, have you?"

"No, no," Tristram smiled. "But you will find them with the angels. And most likely smiling like a pair of fools."

So Tristram led the Count to the castle roof, and there they were, Parson Phineas and Sexton Sam, sacked and singing hosannahs at the top of their lungs.

A grin creased the Count's long face, and he merely reached out his hand. "Your parents will never want; my word on that. Now get out of this realm, young scalawag. If I ever catch you again, you won't trick your way past the rope so blithely."

So Tristram shook his hand and turned on his heel, tripping lightly down the stairs and out of their lives forever.

Or so they thought.

Some use bombs and bravado to boil off their
bile,
Or their lawyers, their hitmen, their gats,
or their mitts.
But a far better style is the guile of a smile.
The most underused weapon we have is our
wits.

16

THE IGUANA PRINCE

nce upon a time, long, long ago, when things were even more unfair than today, this lovely queen gave birth to two daughters, Aurelia and Aurora, and she invited twelve sorceress sisters for tea, hoping each would bestow gifts upon the two princesses. She neglected to invite the thirteenth sister, Maggotine, since the Lady Maggotine was the most waspish woman who ever drew breath.

The affair went swimmingly, the sisters cooing at the twins, chattering, visiting the sumptuous tables to taste the tortes and tarts. But just as the sisters were to offer their gifts, the doors of the chamber slammed open and there stood Maggotine, hardly in a state of bemusement.

Her hair bristled like a bloodthirsty boar, her fiery eyes flashing on either side of her narrow, hairy-warted nose.

"So-o-o-o!" she howled like a cat with her tail in a trap. And she enjoyed it so much she said it again, "So-o-o-o!"

Whisper, whisper, whisper, went her sisters, helpless to stop maniacal Maggotine, as she was the eldest. She strode among them to the table, and with one bash of her wand, she turned the delicacies into swarms of sauteed scorpions, scalloped serpents, and fricasseed frogs. She tasted each, and her awful face smeared into a sour smile of approval.

Then, before anyone could intervene, Maggotine streaked to Aurora's crib and raising her scantling arms shrieked, "I endow you with unsurpassable ugliness, and let it increase day by day!" But as she turned to lay a worse curse on Aurelia, her sisters fell on her like harpies and beat her away with their wands. Maggotine's fury shattered every pane of glass in the palace, and out the gaping casement she flew.

The other sisters turned to tiny Aurora and quickly bestowed all the gifts they could imagine: loving heart, large-mindedness, learning, loyalty, the lot. And they gave Aurelia some of each, too. Finally, the youngest approached Aurora's crib and whispered, "One day, child, you will be happy."

Sick at heart, the young queen nodded them away, then stood at her daughter's crib, watching Aurora growing more unlovely before her very eyes and wondering what "happy" really meant.

The princesses grew, blessed with loving hearts, large-mindedness, learning, and loyalty. Unfortunately, while Aurelia was quite plain, Aurora made even certifiable saints doubt the providence of God. Then one day Aurora heard Aurelia weeping to their royal parents about the embarrassment she was, hidden away like a shameful secret whenever visitors approached, especially young men. She loved Aurora dearly, but . . . So Aurora stepped forward and said, "Let me shut myself up in a tower somewhere, by the sea," she pleaded, "where my hideousness will harm no one. Allow me my nurse and a few servants, and I will go."

The King and Queen made attempts to dissuade her, but in the end they saw the prudence of her proposal. So Aurora retired to a lighthouse where the sea crashed in homage at her feet, and seabirds sang to her, heedless of her face. She painted, embroidered, read books, and spun poems that hymned the hurt in her heart.

One day as she walked a rocky path above the sea, she suddenly stopped in horror. Ahead, under a wind-warped tree, sat a hardly describable creature. He was like a winged iguana the size of a man, his hideous face twisted into knobs and nodules around a tormented mouth and contorted teeth, and his humpbacked body and wings were slick with slimy scales. His fingers speared into talons, his eyes flashed fire, his head haloed in a bristling mane of hair.

"Ah, Princess," the creature cringed with a painful smile. "Yours is not the unpleasantest face or the unhappiest heart."

But Aurora fled in terror to her tower and for days refused to leave, for fear of such another terrifying encounter.

After awhile, she grew restless, and as she walked the beach one evening, she saw a small boat bobbing toward her, a silken sail billowing from its sturdy mast. As it beached at her feet, she saw in the bow a basket of jewels, as if sent as a gift. As she stepped aboard to retrieve it, the boat pulled itself from the beach and began to drift out to sea.

At first, Aurora was frantic. One more of Maggotine's malicious tricks. But as she rode the darkening waves, she felt a sudden surge of peace. How could she change unchangeable truth? What need to dread death? What love could she lose? The only honest compassion she'd had in her life was from a huge iguana, the only creature on earth uglier than she.

But at that moment, overhead, winging through the moonlight came the iguana, settling on the gunnel, his green wings folded against his crooked back. "If you would accept help from someone as fearsome as I," he said shyly, "I am here for you."

Aurora turned away, as saints had done from her. "I . . . ," she choked. "I can't. I can face death more easily than you."

And, grieving, the iguana flew away.

The sea began to heave, and lightning cracked. Thunder rolled overhead, avalanching down on her. Aurora clung to the boat which hurled skyward, then down into dark canyons. Through the spume she spied a ring of rocks around an island, that swiftly surrounded her like giant jaws. With one great heaving wave, her boat crashed against them and split apart. In the flashing dark she fastened her weary arms around what she supposed was the mast, clinging to life even as she dearly longed to let it go.

But the mast began to pull her forward, almost propelled by inner life. And in a flash of lightning Aurora saw she had her arms clutched around the neck of the fearsome iguana-man!

Lightly he laid her by the wall of another lighthouse, and he whispered, "You'd fear me less if you knew me better," and away he flew into the gale.

Aurora fell into exhausted sleep, but when she woke she lay in a downy bed in a room shining in winter light. She hunched up on the bosomy pillows and suddenly caught her breath. Her room was filled with monkeys, smiling in sweet anticipation. But they were all deformed. Some had no legs and humped forward on their hands. Others had no hands but doffed their caps with their feet and bowed. Some had no eyes, no mouths, no ears, but all of them hugged themselves with pleasure in her presence.

"We are here to serve you, Princess," one squinch-faced monkey said, tugging at his single white ear.

For days her minions served her every whim, singing, dancing and playing the weirdest little instruments that nonetheless spun melodies gladdening her heart. They bathed her, dressed her in satin, coiled her hair, clipped diamonds in her ears, chuckled with pleasure at her joy. And throughout the palace, not a single mirror or polished surface that might reflect her face.

"But whose palace is this?" she asked one day.

"Our master's, mum," said the legless lady curling her hair.

"And when will he return?"

"Oh, he's here right now, my lady. He sleeps by day and rises only in dark. Light pains his eyes. But he will wait on you presently, I'm sure."

That very night, as Aurora lay waiting for sleep, she felt a presence in the room and sat up, surprisingly unafraid.

"Ah, princess," a voice said from the dark. "Allow yourself to be loved, and you could find love. Even in hell, honest love cannot die. I am ruler of this realm, and I love you."

Aurora giggled. "Your eyes are poor as your servant said. Truly blind, to love the ugliest woman ever cursed with life."

"But I have seen you," the voice whispered. "And I do adore you. My deepest desire is to see you brimming with happiness."

Aurora's face went slack. "Ah, no. I loved my parents and my sister. My heart won't be wrung like a rag again."

"But perhaps my happiness could ignite yours?" And the voice and the sense of someone present melted into shadows.

From that night on, as she awaited sleep, Aurora also waited her invisible suitor. "I marvel at your strange tastes," she chuckled one evening as they spoke together quietly in dark.

"If loving a woman's heart and not her face is strange, then I am perverse, I suppose." And Aurora felt a soft kiss on her hand and the wetness of the Prince's tears.

"How can I love you if you won't let me see you?" she asked.

"Ah, why make conditions, Princess? Maggotine condemned me, too, to live in darkness seven years. Only one year left. Till then, trust me? Marry me? Would you?"

So, swayed by love—which she'd never known and thus misjudged as pity, she agreed, and the two were wed, and in the dark Aurora felt her damaged friends gamboling and giggling for joy.

For months Aurora was deliriously happy, so happy that she wanted—from joy or spite—to share her happiness with her mother and sister. So, like the unfortunate Psyche, she importuned her husband to allow a visit. Unable to deny her, he agreed, and the two astonished women arrived one day on a royal barge, marveling at the accoutrements of the palace, although their faces pinched when they saw Aurora's outlandish servants, sure some enchantment was working here. And they requested, as delicately as they were able, that Aurora wear a veil when they were speaking together.

Day after day their suspicions grew, and they insisted Aurora wait till her husband was asleep and prove them wrong. "Light a lamp," her mother rasped. "Look! You've been accustomed all your life to ugliness. But for all you know you'll bear a monster's spawn! At least think of those poor distorted children!" And with that they barged back to the palace.

That night, like Psyche before her, Aurora waited till her life's one love was snoring lightly and lit a lamp. But she did not behold handsome Cupid. It was the scaly iguana.

Her prince awoke. "Thus you repay my love?" he cried. "Now I begin my seven years *again!*" And off the wretched fellow flew.

Aurora sank to her knees, sick with grief, and suddenly in a whirl of smoke Maggotine appeared. "Hah!" she screeched. "Your very birth was an insult to me. Now how do I revenge myself for *this* one? Do you think I *enjoy* being ruthless?"

"Madame," Aurora said quietly, "you've been sufficiently revenged for a missing invitation. The gift of ugliness you bestowed on me would more than satisfy anyone less vindictive than you. And now, this cruelty to both my husband and me . . ."

"Curiosity killed the cat," Maggotine barked. "Hm. Well, I . . . No. Can't get soft in my . . . All right," she snorted and whipped out a blob of spiderwebs as big as a beachball. "Spin these to thread, and I may let you pare some time from his sentence." And with a sulphurous whirr, she was gone.

The monkeys came upon the Princess weeping. She poured out her woeful story: the Prince she had betrayed and the price of his return. "I don't even know," she sobbed, "where to find a spinning wheel or how to work one."

"There, there," said the monkeys, and in two snaps the webs had spun themselves onto ten spindles, soft as cream and fine as the hairs on her head.

Next morning when Maggotine erupted in a burst of smoke, she looked at the work and snorted, certain this snip could not have done work so fine. "All right," she snapped, "spin this into a net strong enough to catch a whale, and I might . . . well, we'll see." And she went as swiftly as she'd come.

Again, the monkeys wove Aurora a web from the fragile fibers tough enough to trap a trireme. When Maggotine blew in the following morning, she cast a skeptical eye at the monkeys, who were stepping on their own toes and trying to appear inept, sensing she was being had. *"So-o-o-o!"* she said, without as much acid as she wished. "I must set you a task *no one* can do *for* you. Hm! I have it. Descend to the nethermost bowels of the earth to my cousin, Proserpina, and come back with the essence of wisdom. And the two of you are free." And in a flash she had flown.

Aurora's monkeys were able to help her, but only so far. They led her to a dark cave in the wood and gave her food and a torch, but Maggotine had forbidden them further. So Aurora let herself into the cold darkness and began her torturous trip downward. For what seemed like days she struggled over the rocks, her hands torn and bleeding, pausing to rekindle her torch, sloshing through foul-smelling streams, until finally she came to an enormous cave where victims chained to the rock moaned and wailed in torment. Aurora went from one to the next inquiring where she might find Proserpina, but the prisoners' eyes flared white at the name, and they swooned.

Faint with fatigue, Aurora struggled on. Hours later it seemed, she stopped dead in her tracks. There before her was her iguana Prince, chained hand and foot to the rocks, hardly alive. She ran to a fetid stream and soaked her torn skirt, bringing the water back and squeezing it to his lips, wiping the soot and blood from his haggard, horrible face, rocking him in her arms.

"Ah, my Prince," she sobbed. "I'm not worthy of you. Even my torment since you left hasn't made me worthy."

Slowly, she felt him stir in her arms and turn his frightening face to hers. "You found me," he rasped.

"Yes. Maggotine sent me to find Proserpina, but I can't. So. Let it be. We are together. I will share your prison and your pain. As you said, love can make even hell into heaven."

At that moment, a great shadow fell over them, and they both tensed in terror.

"*What* have we *here!*" The bellow came from a woman with the neck of a bull. Her hair hissed, and her eyes lanced fire at the pair. "Is this . . . *love?*" she screamed. "I simply won't *have* it! Love in hell? Pre*pos*terous!" And she snapped her fingers, and in a flash the Prince and Princess were whirled away, hurled upward through the caverns, and out into the air and light.

Like two fugitives flung from a frightful nightmare, they opened their eyes, and there stood massive Maggotine.

"We-e-e-ell," she snarled, "where is the essence of wisdom? I don't see any flask. If you came back without it . . ."

"The essence of wisdom," said Aurora softly, "is accepting whatever is."

Maggotine's withered hands flew to her heart, and her eyes bulged like balloons. A terrifying cry escaped her lips, and over she went in a heap and withered to dust before their eyes.

The two spells lifted. The Prince did not change into a dashing gentleman, nor did Aurora transform into a ravishing beauty, nor did their monkeys regrow their stunted limbs. The Prince was an ordinary fellow with an engaging grin, and Aurora a girl no man would turn to see again. And their servants had learned long ago to get along quite well with what they had.

But they did live happily ever after, because they finally knew what "happy" meant: accepting whatever is.

Beauty's a ruse that seduces the lover,
A surface deception for children in thrall.
Journey together through hell and discover
True love is the trickiest wisdom of all.

17

GIVE HEED TO THE CLEVER FOX

nce upon a time, long, long ago, when animals often made more sense than those in power, there was this king named Solinus with three sons, Linus, Longinus, and Ninus—whom everyone called Ninny, for such he seemed. Now the reason Solinus could afford to be king was that as a youth he returned from a quest with seeds for a tree that grew golden apples. When they began to ripen, they were meticulously counted each day by the Chancellor of the Exchequer. Suspicion is an occupational disease for kings.

One morning, the Chancellor of the Exchequer charged into the King's chambers crimson and breathless. A golden apple was gone! "Send for the night guard,"

the king hollered. "Off with their heads!" Like suspicion and greed, tenacity is also a qualifier for kingship. They are very royal retainers.

"No, no, Majesty," the old man huffed. "The guards were awake. At exactly midnight, an incredible bird, all covered with golden feathers, lighted on the tree, nipped off an apple and flew away. The guards fired arrows at him but missed."

"Nonsense! The lying thieves made the story up. Off with their heads!" Inflexibility is also a royal requisite.

"No, Majesty! See!" And he held out his hand and there lay a golden feather. "An arrow must have grazed the Golden Bird."

Ah, thought the King, with both tree and bird, he would have a fiscal cushion for the rest of his life. So he sent his oldest son, Linus, in search of this treasure trove.

Next morning Linus set out, cocksure of success, and only a little while after he had entered the forest, he spied a fox sitting by a well. So he cocked his bow and took aim. But to his astonishment, the Fox sat up on his heels and spoke!

"Please, my lord," the Fox said. "Spare my life and I will give you good counsel. By evening, you will reach a village where there are two inns opposite one another. One will be brightly lit and overflowing with raucous laughter and music; the other is quite modest. Go to the modest inn."

Linus grumbled to himself. "Foxes can't talk! Much less give sound advice." So he loosed his arrow. But he missed, and the Fox stretched his legs and tail and streaked away.

As the sun was setting, Linus came to the town, and to his surprise, there were indeed two inns, one filled with exciting music and laughter, the other dingy and small. So without a thought, Linus entered the brightly lit tavern, found a whole group of fascinating friends, and decided to stay awhile.

When months had passed and Linus had not returned, King Solinus sent his second son, Longinus, in search of brother and bird. Longinus met the Fox, received the same dismissable advice, fired and missed, and the Fox streaked off into the forest. Longinus arrived in the village, saw the brightly lit inn with his brother, Linus, making wild wassail within. So he entered the inn and began to savor some high wassail himself, and like his brother, completely lost track of time and task.

More months passed, and Solinus's supply of sons had slowly narrowed to one. Only weak-witted Ninny, who hadn't mastered the art of tying his shoes till he was ten and tended to bump into things with embarrassing regularity. But possession of the Bird had become the King's obsession, so off went Ninus on his quest.

Just inside the wood, Ninny met the Fox, sitting by the well, who begged for his life, even though Ninny had not thought to unshoulder his bow.

"Easy, little Fox," Ninny said. "I mean you no harm."

So the Fox gave Ninny his advice about the inns, and Ninny, sure of his shortcomings and sure that even a fox was wiser than he, thanked him and journeyed on. When he came to the village, he went into the tiny quiet inn and slept a peaceful sleep.

Next morning as he hit the road, there sat the Fox, smiling that at last he'd found a prince with enough wits to take advice.

"Further on," the Fox said, "you will find a castle with a regiment of soldiers standing in the yard. Don't worry. Fast asleep on their feet. Walk right through them; not a sound, mind you. Go into the castle, and in the central salon you will find the Bird in a wooden cage. Take the wooden cage and tiptoe out. Not a sound! And you'll be the heir to the throne."

So Ninny did just as he was told. He came to the castle, saw the soldiers sleeping like statues, tiptoed through and up the stairs, down the corridors and into the central salon. Sure enough, there was the Golden Bird asleep in the wooden cage, and beneath it was the golden apple the bird had stolen. But next to the common cage was a golden cage, all crusted with jewels and a far finer carrier for such a fabulous fowl. So he opened the wooden cage and reached in for the bird, but as he did, the bird woke up and let out a screeching to wake the dead!

Or at least to wake the soldiers dozing in the yard.

Their eyes popped, and they rushed into the castle and seized the nonplussed Ninny. They bound him and dragged him before Leland, lord of that castle. And the Lord, who had a face like a hatchet, leaned down and said: "I feel a bit *mer*ciful today. The sentence is . . . *death!*"

"But . . . but, Your Lordship," Ninny whimpered, "if I'm not mistaken . . . and I often am . . . I believe you mentioned mercy."

"Ye-e-e-es," hissed Lord Leland. "*If* you can bring me the Golden Stallion that outruns the wind! And if you *do* . . . which you probably *can't* . . . you can have the Bird you tried to steal."

"And where might I begin looking, Your Lordship?"

"Hah-ha-*ha!*" said Lord Leland. "That's the hard part."

So sick at heart, as one tends to become under sentence of death and an impossible task, Ninny left the castle and began to wander into the forest. But suddenly before him sat the Fox.

"Didn't I say 'Take the *wooden* cage and tiptoe out'?" the Fox said exasperatedly. "Didn't I say that?"

"Yes," said Ninny. "I'm sorry. I'm not overly attentive."

"All right now. Straight ahead, you'll find another castle. Behind it is the stable. And in the stable is the Stallion. *And* the grooms, but all asleep. Just throw an old saddle on the horse and off you fly. Deliver the horse, pick up the bird, and you'll be the heir to the throne."

So Ninny did as he was told. He found the castle, scooted round to the stable, eased past the sleeping grooms and saw the Stallion. What a noble creature, great muscles coiling under his gilded skin! On the wall hung a leather saddle, cracked and scuffed and all dried out. But on the opposite wall was a saddle befitting this brave beast: gold, with platinum pommel, silver seat, and stirrups of fretwork steel. So Ninny lifted the mythic saddle onto the back of the mythic stallion.

All hell broke loose! The stallion's eyes flared, neighing and battering hooves and shattering stalls fit to wake the dead.

Or at least to wake the sleeping grooms.

They leaped on him, bound him, and hauled him off to Count Conrad, lord of that castle, who sat languidly with one leg over the arm of his throne, trying unsuccessfully to peel a grape.

"Even if I do," he mumbled, "there'll be the bother of the seeds. Well, what is it? Another Stallion rustler? Death!"

"Count Conrad, sir," said the head groom. "He's but a lad."

"Youth is no license for larceny," said the Count and hurled the bothersome grape away and began on another.

"But Your Excellency . . ."

"All right. No need to be tiresome. The sentence holds *unless* your lad brings back my daughter. You know the one."

"Princess Roslyn, sir. She's the only daughter you have."

"Quite," the Count said and dismissed them with a wave.

The groom explained that Countess Roslyn had been spirited away by an aunt rumored to be a witch, on grounds her father was incapable of a girl's upbringing. Actually, the groom whispered, she wanted to replace her brother on the throne and was holding the girl hostage. But when Ninny asked the way, the head groom could only shrug.

Bearing the burden of not one but two death sentences on his young shoulders, Ninny left the castle and wandered into the woods. And to his good fortune, there sat his friend, the Fox.

"I *distinctly* remember saying, 'Throw an *old* saddle on the horse,' " the Fox rasped. "My very words. But *nooo!*"

"I'm sorry," Ninny shrugged. "I'll try better next time."

"There shouldn't *be* a next time, but . . . oh, well. Straight along this path to the aunt's castle. It'll probably take most of the night. In the morning, the Countess comes down to the bathhouse. Run to her and give her a kiss. She hasn't seen a man below ninety since she was two. Leave *right* away. Understand? Don't stop to get ac*quaint*ed, for heaven's sake."

At dawn, his eyes drooling tears of fatigue, Ninny arrived at the palace, and there as promised was lovely Roslyn, walking demurely toward the bathhouse. Her skin was like lilies of the valley, and her sweet face was framed in hair the color of smoke. Ninny was instantly smitten, and he ran to her and planted a long definitive smacker on her rose-petal lips. Her cheeks flushed with rapture, and she returned his kiss avidly, it being her first experience and having no other with which to compare it.

"I am Prince Ninus," Ninny choked. "And I've come to set you free. Come. We must hurry before the servants awaken."

"Oh, Ninus," Roslyn huffed, trying to regain her breath. "I will! I *will!* But first let me tell my maid. I don't want them to think I've been torn to bloody bits by brutish beasts or borne off in unbearable bondage by boorish brigands."

Ninny pleaded. "I have explicit instructions not to dally."

But a crystal tear slid down her perfect cheek. So Ninus relented, and Roslyn skipped gaily off with her ecstatic news.

Mistake. No sooner had Roslyn disappeared within the castle than pandemonium erupted. Footmen came flying from every flank. Ninny was subdued and hauled before the autocratic aunt, whose face seemed assembled from candle drippings of various hues.

"Death!" the vicious whiskered witch hooted, which had become nearly natural for Ninny. *"But* I've been annoyed at an unsightly hill that hinders my view of the swamps. If you move that before dawn," she cackled, "I shall give you my niece as a reward. *Bonne chance,"* she said, for she was not uncultured.

Ninny dragged his sleepless carcass out and began to dig, and dig, and dig some more. But finally he fell on his back and lamented to the moon, "This is it, then."

But right at his ear crouched the Fox. " 'Take her *right* away,' I said. But *noooo!* What are you doing out here in the middle of the night? Don't even tell me. The old bird wants the mound removed, yes? All right. Get some sleep."

So, scarcely out of obedience, Ninny fell into a stupor.

When he awoke, the mound was gone.

He leaped to his feet and ran to the wicked witch, and like it or not, Countess Roslyn was his. So the boy and girl set forth, and it was not long before friend Fox made an appearance.

"First, take the Countess back to the Count. There'll be great rejoicing. They'll bring her Golden Stallion out for her. Mount as fast as you can, both of you, and gallop away. No one will catch you, for it runs swifter than wind."

So this time, Ninny followed instructions perfectly and made off with Countess Roslyn, who thought he was the greatest *man* she'd ever known, and with the Golden Stallion as well.

As they raced away, they encountered the Fox once more. "Now," he said, "when you come to the castle of the Golden Bird and they bring her out, keep the reins in one hand and reach for the bird with the other. Then hop back onto the Golden Stallion and off you go, and you'll be the heir to the throne. Oh, yes. One last thing: Don't buy any gallows' flesh and avoid wells."

Puzzling over those last two admonitions, off they rode on the Golden Stallion. Who would want to buy the flesh of a man who'd been hanged? And what was wrong with wells? But Ninny put that out of his mind and again carried out instructions to the letter. And off he rode with horse and bird and bride.

As they were trotting blissfully through the village where Ninny had stayed the night, they saw that two men were about to be hanged. Ninny reined in at the foot of the gallows and suddenly saw that the two prisoners were his own brothers!

"But what are they charged with?" he asked the hangman.

"Drunk and disorderly conduct," he said. "Gambling, destruction of property, and making improper proposals to the mayor's wife. That last one was the kicker."

Ninny reached into the cage and took out the golden apple. "Would you trade them for this?" And the hangman was not at all averse to that and quickly handed over the wastrel brothers, and off they set for home, happy and free.

But when they came to the well where each had met the Fox, the brothers suggested a stop to rest and slake their thirst. So of course while Ninny was retailing his adventures, he heedlessly sat on the edge of the well. With a whoop, the brothers shoved him in, and off they sped with Golden Bird and Golden Stallion and Golden Girl. But once home, the Stallion would not eat, the Bird's feathers began to dim, and Roslyn did nothing but weep, for the brothers swore, if she betrayed them, they would feed her heart to the Golden Bird and the rest to the Golden Stallion.

Meanwhile, Ninny was sloshing around in the well, sure he would drown since he could neither swim nor scale its slippery sides. Just as he was about to say his final prayers, he looked up, and there was the snout of the Fox.

"Your mother was inspired when she named you, my friend," said the Fox. "Watch out. I'm sending down a bucket." So the Fox lowered a bucket on a rope he grasped in his strong teeth and slowly hauled the sodden Ninny back up to the forest floor.

"You're not out of the woods yet," the Fox said. "As you travel down the road, find a beggar. Exchange your clothes for his, and you can enter without your brothers knowing."

So Ninny did as he was told and entered the castle grounds in shredded stinking clothes. No one knew him. But suddenly in the palace, the Golden Bird brightened and began to sing. The Golden Stallion was willing to eat. And Countess Roslyn felt a sudden rush in her heart. King Solinus marveled at this wondrous change and summoned the countess to him, demanding to know what was going on. And finally she told him the whole story.

And how she sensed, somehow, her true bridegroom was near.

"Somewhere out there," she said, casting her gaze out the casement. And at that moment, she saw him! Running down to the courtyard, she threw her arms around him. And all was well.

King Solinus banished the two wicked brothers, Ninny and Roslyn were wed, and King Ninus the First sought out his Fox and made him Lord Chief Justice, Chancellor of the Exchequer, Keeper of the Privy Purse, and Lord High Everything Else.

If one tends not to be overly attentive,
Just stick to instructions; don't try to be
inventive.
The lesson learned at the College of Hard
Knocks is:
If your wits are weak, leave thinking to the
Foxes.

18

THE INVISIBLE WORM

 nce upon a time, long, long ago, when virtue was its own reward and punishment, there lived this very noble but quite financially strapped Duke Benedict, who was blessed with three lovely daughters, Astrid, Augusta, and Althea. The Duke dithered a great deal over dowries, not to mention whether they could afford dinner from day to day. Yet he truly could not complain.

Astrid, the youngest, was a woman so stunning and statuesque that suitors and sculptors lined up for half a league outside their crumbling castle just for a glimpse of her. She was not only comely but superbly athletic as well, having humiliated most of the he-men in the kingdom more than once at the javelin, mace, and broadsword. She would make a superb match someday and perhaps alleviate the Duke's catastrophic cash flow.

Augusta, though of somewhat forbidding mien and physique, had a mind like a whirlwind, sucking up, synthesizing and spewing forth ideas more swiftly than the palace scribes could scribble them down. Her salon was clogged with scruffy scholars hoping to squeeze a dissertation from her random thoughts. Some great king, one day, would sue for her hand, if only to keep her from advising other kings, and the family's financial fears could be forgotten. But Augusta did not suffer fools with much grace, and as a result her adoring audience changed with some frequency.

The charitable might say that Althea, the eldest, was pretty, in a quite ordinary kind of way. She it was who charmed the provender purveyors, pig butchers, and process servers and who handled the more pedestrian chores of the run-down castle: cajoling the few servants to work past the point of exhaustion, conjuring feasts for the wealthy suitors so artfully flavored and presented that none could tell they were possum and woodchuck, and in general making a penny work as hard as a pound.

Ordinarily, Althea was too busy to think too much of her own prospects. But when she did find five minutes to sit in a corner of the steaming kitchen and fan her drenched brow and bosom, whispers of envy wafted through the back rooms of her mind. If only she were as beautiful and buxom as Astrid or as wise and witty as Augusta. But there was not much time for such envious thoughts. Still, the envy lay there, deep in her soul, like a worm in a bright-cheeked apple.

Another one of Althea's chores, owing to the strain on the supply of servants, was to act as chaperone when one of her sisters had vaguely focused on a potential beau and consented to see the young cavalier alone. Although Astrid and Augusta were sensitive to the family's fiscal fix, they did perversely insist that their intendeds be not just world-class wealthy but also heart-breakingly handsome, superbly shaped, and wittily diverting. That did, of course, ease somewhat the burden of winnowing the swarm of suitors who queued up daily at the gates.

One day Astrid was entertaining Duke Derek of Dabney, whose face and form were as streamlined a Grecian statue and whose chiseled cheeks and chin framed a porcelain grin. Althea sat quietly in a corner knitting and trying to dream up recipes to enhance the flavors of snake and grass, only half-listening to the prittle-prattle of biceps and triceps and stepover toeholds.

"Tut, tut, sir," Astrid purred, "I believe the term 'varsity' arises from the fact that each member of the team must specialize in one of various roles."

"Forgive me, my lady," Derek grinned, "but mightn't it be that such a group has a variety of tricks and ploys to deflate their opponent's advantages?"

"Perhaps," Althea said from her bored half-stupor, "the word comes from the fact that only young boys have the time and freedom from duty to play at such children's games, and they do it at what the common folk call the 'univarsity'?"

Astrid and Derek swung their perfect faces at the young woman they had forgotten in the corner.

"I do believe your sister's right," Duke Derek agreed.

But Astrid lasered a look at her sister that would have sliced through granite.

Another day Augusta was bantering with Baron Bertrand of Bostwick of the metaphysical music of the spheres, the disputed claims of alchemy, and speculation of spontaneous generation, while Althea sat unnoticed, darning Augusta's stockings and hatching schemes to outwit the egg farmer.

"Fie, my dear Baron," Augusta chortled, "that a man of your obvious attainments should think such a thing about women."

"Ah, my dearest Lady Augusta," Baron Bertrand beamed, "I meant no insult to *your* obvious attainments. It's just that—to the Great Unwashed among whom we are so lamentably awash—a woman's proper function is to run the household, hostess her master's parties, and civilize the children."

Althea shifted in her chair. "Which doesn't mean she doesn't have a mind," she said and rethreaded her needle. "You don't feed a family on the music of the spheres."

"Well, I, uh . . . ," Baron Bertrand huffed inconclusively.

But Augusta skewered Althea with a scowl that would have melted a mirror.

It came to pass, however, that in the musty damp of the castle, Duke Benedict caught a mild case of the sniffles that, combined with the drafts that whinnied through the stone corridors like a herd of mustangs, quickly devolved into pneumonia during which the poor old man's brittle bones rattled like a xylophone playing a Mozart fugue, till finally, in one heroic chord, he took his leave to continue his efforts among the celestial choirs. In short, he died.

In the absence of the male heir whom Lady Astrid or Lady Augusta and their not-yet-chosen consorts had been expected to provide, the Royal Council was in a bit of a tizzy. It was something short of shocking that the Duke's only progeny were—face the facts—female. The counselors tutted and muttered to one another, sagely, about the unsuitability of a sovereign like Lady Astrid who, though admittedly a catch for any king, seemed to have a world-view narrowed to the scope of an Indian club. Lady Augusta, on the other hand, was intimidatingly erudite, yet the Council balked at finding themselves in the position of offering advice to someone who already had all the answers. Or at least thought she did. Which left only Lady Althea, who after all was the eldest. Despite her dishpan hands. And her waspish temper. But the girl did have common sense. And surely she would need no lectures on balancing the budget.

So, amid modified jubilation, Duchess Althea was crowned and took her place at the center of the ducal court. At first, she was better acquainted with the names and functions of chimney sweeps then of her chancellors, but she was a bright woman and soon caught on. And she had a lifetime of learning how to get what she wanted done. Gradually she saw that, *mutatis mutandis,* running a duchy was little different from running a household. The egos were larger, more obstinate, and more bruisable, yet just as persuadable when the choice was agreement or unemployment. The duchess was perfectly capable of running her domain.

But not the household, too.

So she summoned her sisters to a private meeting in what had once been the Duke's apartments. Astrid and

Augusta sat sipping their tea and peering judgmentally—not to say enviously—over the rims of their cups, expecting to be instructed to marry some bibulous boor with an exorbitant bank account.

"All right," Althea said with her customary forthrightness, "I never asked to rule, but I have it, and that's that. But I can't keep one eye on chancellors charging their soirees to the exchequer and the other on potboys pilfering potatoes. You're going to have to help me."

Astrid and Augusta looked at one another as if their elder sister had just suggested they sit to supper with serfs. Then they looked at her.

"What," asked Augusta cautiously, "did you have in mind?"

"Astrid takes charge of the household; Augusta takes charge of the castle finances."

Neither of her sisters could muster the breath to say, "What?" once more.

"Well?" Althea said. "I'm not really asking your permission. If you want to eat, you have to work."

A great tear pearled down Astrid's perfect cheek, and Augusta tried to assume a great height but failed.

"Well?" Althea scowled. "What is it?"

"It was always *you,*" Astrid sniffed.

Augusta snorted away her own tears. "Yes. She's right. You were always the one."

"What?" said Althea. "*I* was the one? I mended your drawers and drew your baths and faked your feasts! *I* was the one? Oh yes. The stupid one. The plain one. The oh-you-can-count-on-old-Althea one! And the two of you strutted around like perfumed peacocks! Oh, yes. I was the one, all right. The fool."

"It was you father loved," Astrid said grimly.

"Ho-*ho*, a fine way to show *love!* I was an unpaid steward, governess, housekeeper, dietician, drudge . . . And you two . . ."

"Yes," sighed Augusta. "We were the perfumed peacocks. Pawns. Pampered properties. Dispensable. He couldn't wait to get rid of us. But he'd never have let you go."

Althea stared at them, unable to comprehend.

Astrid snickered. "And all our beaux? They always left saying, 'My, isn't your sister Althea a wise woman?' "

"Yes," Augusta laughed humorlessly. " 'She'd make a fine wife and mother,' they always said. 'A fine queen.' "

Althea's two sisters turned to her, suddenly beginning to comprehend.

"Althea," Astrid stammered, "you weren't . . ."

"Oh, no. You weren't jealous of *us,*" Augusta gasped.

"But . . . ," Althea began but couldn't think what to say.

"How many times," Astrid sniffed, "I was honestly ready to take a razor to my cheeks. If only someone could look at me for myself and not for my face, my physique, my ability to leap like a clever seal. Everyone always looked at you as just . . . you."

"Astrid and I have talked about it a great deal," Augusta said, brushing away a tear. "I could spin out all kinds of celestial calculus. But I couldn't spin. I could touch people's heads, but not their hearts."

"You don't mean . . . ?"

"That we were jealous of you?" Astrid smiled. "Of course."

"No, I . . ."

For a moment, all three sisters merely looked, astonished, at one another. Then they flung themselves together. And with great pain, they forgave one another for who they were.

And later, they even forgave themselves.

> *We'd all be rather happy, if that were our*
> *   honest aim.*
> *Yet we envy others' assets and esteem,*
> *And trade our light for dark, and we turn our*
> *   pride to shame—*
> *While the others aren't as happy as they seem.*

19

THE WAY PEARLS ARE MADE

nce upon a time, long, long ago, when wisdom was harder to avoid, there lived this old, old woman named Dagmar, in a little cottage in a remote clearing in the mountains. Her face was fierce as a pitbull's, but even though she had to hobble about on a crutch, she was always cheerful, roving the meadows for grass for her geese and wild fruit for herself and her unfortunate stepdaughter, Gloam. Although many years younger than her stepmother, Gloam looked as old. A great tall girl, grizzled hair spiked out from a most unlovely face, warted and wan.

One day as Dagmar sickled grass by the side of the road to the town, she spied a fine young man sauntering along enjoying the birdsong and the sigh of the soft breeze in the trees.

"Good day, Your Highness," Dagmar cackled, for surely a man so finely dressed must be at least a grand duke.

"Ah, no, old mother," the young man said, opening a fine white smile. "Only the son of a count, though an unfairly rich count, to be sure. My name is Conor. And I seem irretrievably lost. My, that sack looks awfully heavy for a frail old lady."

"Well, each takes the burden we're given. Mine is to be a peasant. Grass for my geese, wild apples for my stepdaughter and me. You going *that* way?" she asked, pointing away from the town.

"Is that the way to the town?" Conor asked.

"It could be," Dagmar smiled. "That's the way I'm going."

"Then, let me carry your sack a ways," the young man said.

"That would be kind, child," Dagmar chuckled and transferred the heavy load onto the young man's back and cinched it on with knots very cunningly fastened.

"This *is* heavy," Conor grunted. "It's a wonder you could even lift it, old as you are."

"Hardly an hour from here," she said and limped ahead.

"An hour! Already this feels like it's filled with cobblestones!" And he tried to set it down, but Dagmar had tied it so craftily that, turn and twist as he might, he couldn't shuck it off. It was if it were growing from between his shoulder blades.

On they trudged, and on some more. The pack was painfully heavy on level ground, but after about a half-hour, Dagmar snorted, "To the right now," and blinded by his own sweat, Conor realized they were starting to climb, the stones rolling and sifting from under his feet as if they were alive and spiteful.

"Mother," Conor gasped, "I have to rest!"

"It *is* getting a bit much, isn't it?" she wheezed. "But if you stop, you'll go stiff. I'll give you a fine reward."

Conor's knees trembled like jelly, and his clothes were sodden with sweat. "Old woman," he groaned, "you're shameless!"

"True," she said and began to belabor his calves with a switch, as if he were a big-hammed ox.

Finally, they arrived at her cottage, and Conor sank to his knees, breathless, pain rocketing through every limb and even aching his teeth. He felt the burden lifted and wrenched his sleeve across his forehead to sponge the sweat. When he opened his eyes, he saw a huge, grotesque woman approaching in the midst of a gaggle of geese, honking and slapping their wings and craning their necks with glee at their mistress's return.

"Mother," said the gangling girl, "I worried!"

"Not a bit of it, Gloam," Dagmar cackled. "No, this fine young man, Sir Conor, helped me carry my sack. Oh, young Conor, this is my stepdaughter, Gloam. Just sit by the door and rest. We'll fetch you something cool. And I must give you your reward. Come, Gloam. Not fitting a young lass like yourself be alone with a young gentlemen. He might fall in love with you."

Conor doubted the likelihood of that, and he lay exhausted on a bench and looked over the vale, green and fresh, late sun sparkling on a giggling brook, and he fell asleep awhile.

"Now, then," Dagmar squawked and handed him a beaker of ice-cold water. "I've treated you ill, but you didn't die of it, did you? If you're son of a count, you've no need of money nor land, but here is something." And she thrust into his hand a tiny box that looked as if cut from a single emerald. "Guard it well," Dagmar smiled. "It will bring you good fortune."

So Conor, surprising even himself, leaped to his feet as fresh as a boy from his bed, sure of some magic in the water.

"When you reach the road," she sniggered, "turn the *other* way. That's the way to town. I fear I deceived you a touch."

So Conor made his way down the hill and finally reached the town after dark. When the watchman heard his name, he bade him enter and took him at once to the palace. The King and Queen were about to retire, but when they heard a nobleman was seeking succor, they agreed to meet him in the hall. As Queen Constance approached, Conor fell on his knee and held out the emerald box.

She took it in her delicate fingers and pried open the lid. For a moment her sleek face went slack, but her eyes went wide, and she took a great breath and fainted to the floor.

The courtiers fell on Conor and began to drag him away to dungeons, but the Queen gave a tiny gasp and came to her senses in the King's arms. "No," she whispered. "Release him! Please! Leave us. I must speak with this young man alone."

Reluctantly, King and courtiers departed, and the Queen led Conor to a small room and bade him sit next to her. She dried her tears and composed herself.

"I had three daughters," she said quietly. "Delia, Delilah, and Dawn. Delia and Delilah were the oldest. Difficult girls. Always backbiting, scheming. But Dawn. Ah, Dawn was an apple blossom, radiant as sunbeams. She hardly cried, no matter how cruel her sisters were. But when she wept, it was a single tear, and that tear became a pearl." For a moment, the Queen became distract. "I wonder, have you heard of King Lear?" When

Conor nodded, the Queen continued. "When Dawn was fifteen, King Quentin summoned our daughters and proposed Lear's foolish question. 'Daughters,' he said, 'Today I decide who will receive what parts of my realm and wealth. I know you all love me, but whichever loves best will fare the best.'

"Well, Delia spoke first. 'Oh, Papa!' she simpered, 'I love you more than sun, moon and stars. Better than Venus, Mars . . . ,' and she would have named more, had she been brighter. Then Delilah spoke, like honeyed vinegar: 'Daddy dearest! I love you more than life, more than bread, wine, meat, or sugar gumdrops!' Enough to make one ill. Then Dawn spoke, 'Father,' she said, her tiny chin thrust out, 'I know not how to answer. Love is love.' But the King pressed, and finally she said, 'Nothing in life has taste without salt. I love you as I love salt.'

"My husband is something of a literalist, which can make things difficult. 'Salt!' he cried. 'Then you shall be paid in salt!' So in his fury, he divided the kingdom between Delia and Delilah. But he bound a sack of salt around Dawn's neck and had her driven into the forest. We pleaded and prayed, but he would not budge. Of course, before a week went by he repented his anger, but when he sent soldiers to find our daughter, they found nothing. Only a few pearls by the side of the road. I can only hope she found a touch of shelter and compassion."

For a moment, Queen Constance was silent. Then she opened the box and handed it to Conor. Within, there was a single teardrop pearl. "You must tell me how you came by this pearl."

So Conor told her the whole story about Dagmar and how she rewarded him with the emerald box. The Queen rose and said that, if he would be so kind as to lead them, she and the King would go with him on the morrow and seek out this Dagmar. If she knew of the pearl, she might have some news of her daughter.

Meanwhile, that same evening, Dagmar sat spinning by the dying fire in her mountain cottage. She heard the geese fussing and honking near the door, and a moment later Gloam came in and stacked some wood by the hearth. Wordlessly, the ungainly girl sat staring into the embers. Suddenly there was a scratching at the window, and two fiery yellow eyes peered in. A great owl sat there and huffed, "Uh-hoo!" three times and away he flew.

Dagmar looked up at the big young woman and nodded. "Follow the owl, my dear," she said softly. Gloam arose and went out, like a woman mesmerized. She crossed the meadow and climbed up into a shadowy valley till she came to a glen where a well sat in a circle of three old oaks. Finally, the moon rose, a circle of silver, and shouldered over the mountain, so bright you could have found a pin. And there sat the owl, bidding her nearer. Gloam came and buried her hands in the water of the well and sloshed it over her face. And she was transformed!

The grey flesh of her face melted and smoothed till her skin was like apple blossom, and her bright hair burst forth like sunbeams. Her eyes shone. She moved about in the moonlight, fresh and fair, till she was breathless with delight.

But then there was a crackling high up in the oaks, and the owl huffed "Uh-hoo!" and drifted away into dark. The maiden froze like a doe, and at that moment, a cloud covered the moon, and darkness spread through the glade once more. And her beauty vanished like a candle blown out in the wind. And there hulked the giantess Gloam once more.

She ran home, her nerves like aspen leaves, and Dagmar met her by the door and led her into the house and sat her by the fire. "It's three years to the day that you came to me," the old lady said. "Tomorrow is the day." And she rose and grasped a broom and began sweeping the floor.

"But mother," Gloam said. "It's nearly midnight."

"Yes," Dagmar hissed. "I must leave everything right. I must leave you tomorrow."

The big girl was in panic. "But . . ."

"Have no fear, child. You will always have a roof. I have left a silken gown in your room. Go to bed. Sleep well."

But earlier that same evening, Conor had been restless and decided to reconnoiter the road ahead, sure that the following day he could bring King and Queen to Dagmar's cottage. As he turned off the road at the spot he suspected she had led him up the pebbled hill, a dark shape swept over his head, and he ducked as it flew past huffing "Uh-hoo." As he crested the hill into the meadow, he saw an ungainly shape slip from the cottage door.

"Ha!" Conor said to himself. "The great goose-girl, Gloam. Probably out to meet the old witch for a coven." So as quietly as he could, he followed the hulking shape up the valley into a small glen formed by three great oaks. He climbed one and sat in its branches, watching as she dipped her great coarse hands in the well. To his astonishment, she turned in the sudden moonlight, radiant and transformed. He hardly dared breathe, and he reached to part the branches further. But he overreached himself, and the branch cracked. The owl flapped hooting away. The moon suddenly disappeared. And the girl was gone.

Next morning, as daylight began to paint the sides of the mountain, Conor woke and wended his way toward the cottage, sure now of what he would find. As he did, he saw the King and Queen and their retinue following his trail up through the meadow. He ran to them and told them what he'd seen the night before.

The party waited behind as the three approached the cottage, where the geese still dozed, snouts under their wings. Inside, they saw shriveled Dagmar quietly spinning at her wheel in her spanking clean room. When they tapped on the window, she looked up smiling, as if she expected them. She opened the door. "Come in," she said kindly, but when they sat she skewered the King with agate eyes. "You might have spared yourself the jaunt if your arrogance hadn't driven away a child more honest than milk."

The King hung his head and said into his beard, "A stupidity of which my shame has reminded me these three years. She has a good heart. If only there's enough space to encompass me."

"All right, then. Come out now, child," said Dagmar.

And from the bedchamber came Princess Dawn arrayed in silk, her golden hair brimming and her eyes wet with tears. She ran to her mother and embraced her, then turned to her shame-faced father. "Father," she said, and embraced him without another word.

"My child," King Quentin said, wiping away his own tears, "I've given away my kingdom. What have I left for you?"

"She'll want for nothing," Dagmar cackled and opened a stout little chest, dazzling them with light. "I've saved her tears."

"Then my cruelty," King Quentin said, "gave you something."

"And she has my little house," Dagmar said, and in a whirlwind she disappeared from sight.

The house rocked with the force of her passing. Everything in the cottage tore from its moorings and reeled round the room. The King and Queen and Dawn and Conor were hurled to the floor, clinging to one another.

And when everything settled, they opened their eyes, and the hovel had turned into a splendid palace. The floors were marble, and the windows hung with rainbow tapestries through which the morning sun was streaming. The doorway opened, and one after another young women in white moved forward and encircled the bewildered royals. The geese had been released from their spell, too, the other young girls old Dagmar had kept from harm when their parents had treated them cruelly.

And all, once again, was well.

Don't expect all your tears will transform
    into pearls.
Even stories restrict that to ladies and earls.
Yet for peasant's pain the gods don't forbid some
Reward: that our tears sometimes turn
    into wisdom.

20

CURIOUS QUIZZICAL, CURIOUS QUEER

nce upon a time, long, long ago, when con-formity was the norm and curiosity an aberration, there was this boy named Digby. But they called him Digger, because he was always trying to figure out how things work and what they're for. His favorite word was "why." But he lived in a grey town where people had serious, dead-ended faces as if they all had terminal acid stomach and toothaches. So whenever Digger asked, "Why?" they'd snap, "That's the way we've *always* done it" or "It's compulsory" or "It's forbidden." So, as you can imagine, they all thought Digger pretty curious. Not just inquisitive. Downright weird.

Well, one day there came to town a strange old beggar with laser-beam eyes and a glow all round him, like he was radioactive or something. His cloak was a tangle of tatters and his battered hat like a blackbird's nest. And his indifference to personal hygiene was evident in his eye-crossing smell. Naturally, the townsfolk turned up their collars and bustled about their business. Who wants to complicate their lives with a loony? But Digger went right up to the old codger, tugged at his raggedy sleeve, and asked the question of all questions: "Please, sir," he said, "what are people for?"

A rainbow smile smeared across the old man's face. "Ah," he sighed, "at *last!* 'What are people for?' Yep, that's the only question all right!" And he reached in his coat and pulled out a map covered with mysterious symbols and runes. "All right, young fella, you've got to find your way to Castle Heder. Meet the three weird sisters." And before Digger could close his gaping jaws for another question, the old man was gone like smoke.

Digger sat on a milestone awhile and puzzled over the curious chart, none too sure he even had it right side up. All the words were in some cryptic code, but fortunately there were pictures as well, some none too welcoming: griffins with great hawk heads and wide warped wings, dragons with flinty fangs fluming flame, and other beasties he could not put a name to but whose acquaintance he would prefer to spare himself.

So off Digger went, clutching his map, and that's when his troubles began. Which, of course, is what a quest is for.

A few hours outside the village, Digger came upon a dense wood crowded with craggy outcrops of rock. And as he pawed his way through the brush, he came upon a griffin, perched on a boulder, his cruel eyes lancing from either side of a silver beak. Unaware at first of Digger's presence, the griffin sat idly picking his formidable teeth, and at his taloned feet lay a bloody lionskin, recently emptied. Then Digger caught his feral attention, and his eyes skewered him.

"Excuse me, Sir Griffin," Digger said, doffing his cap. "I'm searching for the Castle Heder."

"Haven't the slightest," the Griffin said and belched.

"You see, I'm trying to find what people are for."

"Well, then," the Griffin said with what seemed a smile, "I can spare you the trip. People are for eating." He cast a disdainful glance at the empty lionskin. "Much more tasty than beasts. Fortunately for you, I've reached satiety. Hm," he said, eyeing Digger up and down. "No more than an hors d'oeuvre at best. Still, you ought to be on your way. I have quite marvelous metabolism."

So as quickly as he could, Digger took his leave and plunged back into the forest. For hours, he pushed onward, one tree looking exactly like the one he'd just passed, which made him wonder if he weren't traveling in circles. And he dearly wished he'd stopped at home before he set out and packed a lunch.

Then suddenly he broke through the trees and found himself face to face with a cliff, and at its feet a long line of great hairy men with slave-slack faces trudged toward what seemed a cave, and another line stumbled out of it, laden with great rocks glinting with streaks of gold. Along the line paced a tiny fellow with a scrunched-up face and orange hair spuming from his wrinkled brow. The troll scowled and cracked his whip on the prisoners' legs and shouted, "Faster, you louts! Only work can set you free! You're nowhere near half your quota for the day. If you don't get moving, I'll double it! Move! Move! Move!"

Digger was about to scoot back into the brush, but the little fellow was his only hope. So he buckled his courage and clambered across the fallen rocks and cleared his throat. The troll turned and scowled him up and down.

"Too small," he snarled. "Go away."

"Excuse me, sir. I . . . I'm looking for the Castle Heder."

"Waste of time," and he turned back to lashing his whip.

"But I'm looking to find what people are for."

"Foolish question. Answer's obvious. Just look," and he pointed to the slave lines. "People are to work. All those hide-bags of bones have hired themselves to us for gold. Hah! You feel sorry for them? Knee-jerk silly. If we knocked off their chains and set them free, they'd beg us to shackle them up again. They know that after twenty years we'll set them free with enough gold to retire to the South Seas. If they survive."

"Please, sir. Castle Heder?"

"Oh, it's over there somewhere," the Troll said, batting his hand in the general direction of the west.

"Thank you, sir," Digger said and turned to take his leave.

"Start lifting things!" the Troll shouted after him. "Build up those arms and legs. We have no use for spindleshanks!"

For hours more, Digger plodded on till he broke out of the forest onto a broad green plain. A stream wove through its flowered flanks and silvered in the setting sun. At the center sat a huge castle, its turrets shafting up into the dying light.

Digger made his way across the grassy meadows and over the heavy drawbridge. He reached up his fist and rapped on the big oaken door. Slowly it swung back and framed a stern-faced giantess with iron-grey hair and spectacles the size of barrel hoops. " 'Bout time," she snapped. "You must be Digger. Old Solon said you might be by. Name's Dame Verity. Sounds like 'charity.'

'S not. Nowhere near the same thing. Charity's m'sister. You're not ready for her yet. So. Hop to it." And she led Digger into a room big as the Goodyear Blimp Hangar, piled floor to roof with junk: astrolabes, Geiger counters, boxes and boxes of chemicals, Bunsen burners, and what looked like all the parts to several atomic reactors. Among other oddments. "Well, sort it out. Off you go," Verity said, and off she went to fix their supper.

So Digger dug in, setting the place to rights, separating things that looked alike, putting up shelving, asking Verity everything's name and what it was for, dusting, oiling, washing, polishing, till the place looked like the Sloan-Kettering Institute. "Dandy," Verity snorted. "You're ready for my sister, Charity, now." So she gave him a bag of peanut butter sandwiches and sent him off down the road.

When he finally got to the end, Digger found a beautiful park around a lake that glistened like silver, and at the gate a sweet little old lady like Billie Burke in "The Wizard of Oz," but not so much Maybelline. "Hello, dear," she smiled. "Come in, Digger." So Digger followed into the park but stopped in his tracks. That beautiful place was filled with limping fawns, and broken-winged birds, and rickety little boys, and misshapen little girls. Digger's heart felt bruised, and he looked up at Dame Charity. "Yes, dear," she said. "Aren't they beautiful?" Digger stammered, "But . . . why?" Her tiny brows pinched. "Oh," she said, "Why are they like that? So we can love them, dear."

So Digger began shyly to nod at the broken animals and children, and gradually he began to smile at them, and talk to them, and to hold their twisted hooves and shaky hands, and to look deeply in their knowing, grateful eyes. He did tricks and sang songs in his silly breaking voice, and soon they were all laughing and trying to bring their clumsy hands together to clap for him. And Digger had never been happier in his life. But one day Dame Charity came to him and said, "It's time to move on, Digger." He pleaded, but she assured him he could come back; now he had to make the final stop at Fortress Fearless.

So off Digger whistled till he came to a great bulwark with a moat, crossed the drawbridge and hammered on the big door. It creaked open, and there stood this bolster-bosomed giant lady in a sweatsuit with a whistle around her Old Sequoia neck. "Well, Digger!" she bellowed. "Come in and meet my kids." And she led him into a big yard, where all these intimidatingly fit boys and girls were leaping and cavorting like a herd of kangaroos on cannabis, and she introduced each one: Patience, Bravura, Moxie, Paladin, Appassionata, Will, and a host more, including the runt of the litter, Spunk, and his Jewish cousin, Chutzpah.

So for a month, Digger joined them in their training games: Stand-Up-and-Be-Counted, Keep-the-Ol'-Chin-Up, Stick-Your-Neck-Out, Beard-the-Lion-in-His-Den, Take-the-Bull-by-the-Horns, Bell-the-Cat, and Put-Your-Self-on-the-Line. Till finally one day, Digger was summoned to the gate where they waited for him: Verity, and Charity, and their big sister, Tenacity. "It's time, Digger. You're ready. Now you know what people are for."

"But," Digger stammered, "what am I s'posed t'do?"

The three sisters smiled. "When it happens, you'll know. From now on, it's all improvisation." So Digger trudged glumly up the path. But the Three Weird Sisters called out, "Don't worry, Digger. You're filled with magic now." So Digger smiled, and stuck out his chin, and climbed on up the road, whistling.

> *Our schools prepare our young to live*
> *"The Good Life," K-thru-12, and well beyond*
>   *their teens.*
> *One wonders why they never give*
> *At least the slightest hint at what "Good Life"*
>   *means.*